THE STORY OF LOWESTOFT

Part 2 1877 - 1924

by

Jack Mitchley

edited by Stuart Jones BA and William Keith

Also by Jack Mitchley:

THE STORY OF LOWESTOFT LIFEBOATS Part 1 1801-1876

(First published by the Port of Lowestoft Research Society 1973)
(Second Edition published by Lowestoft Libraries 1975 ISBN 0 904328 00 7)

PLRS007/1000

ISBN 0 9505311 3 8

British Library Cataloguing in Publication Data.
A catalogue record for this book is available from the British Library.

Published by: THE PORT OF LOWESTOFT RESEARCH SOCIETY,
                LOWESTOFT, SUFFOLK.

Printed by: Tyndale Press Ltd, Lowestoft, Suffolk

CONTENTS

Cover photo: RNLB *Samuel Plimsoll* (ON22) being launched off the North beach at Lowestoft during the 1892 Lifeboat Trials. (PLRS collection)

FOREWORD

It is both a great privilege and a great pleasure to be invited to write the Foreword to Part 2 of The Story of the Lowestoft Lifeboats.

I first got to know Jack Mitchley nearly thirty years ago when I was appointed Station Honorary Secretary of Lowestoft Lifeboat. I can picture Jack all those years ago even now. He seldom missed a service by the Lowestoft Lifeboat. In those days the Lifeboat's moorings were in Hamilton Dock. How well I can recall Jack's figure mounted on his cycle with camera slung over his shoulder, pedalling along Hamilton Road after the maroons had been fired.

Jack was always kindness itself and his unfailing courtesy is an example to all who knew him. I well remember that shortly after my appointment Jack presented me with a set of pictures of all the Lowestoft Lifeboats. They were beautifully mounted in two frames. I treasure them to this day.

Part 1 of the Story of Lowestoft Lifeboats was published in 1974 and covered the period 1801 - 1876. Jack wrote the book with painstaking accuracy. His untimely death on 21 June 1993 prevented the publication of Part 2 covering the period 1877 - 1924. However, before his death Jack had been working on the book. I need hardly say that his notes were meticulous.

After Jack's death Stuart Jones and William (Billy) Keith set to work to complete and edit Jack's second volume. Not only can this book be seen as a tribute to Jack and his meticulous work but it is the authoritative work covering the history of Lowestoft Lifeboats over the period.

Stuart and Billy, himself a member of the Lowestoft Lifeboat crew for many years, have done a wonderful job and I have no hesitation in commending their work to those whose interests focus on the sea and to those who wish to explore the history of one of Britain's oldest lifeboat stations.

Michael W Chapman
October 1995

INTRODUCTION

In 1974 the late Jack Mitchley published Part 1 of The Story of Lowestoft Lifeboats. It covered the early years of the station from 1801 for a period of 75 years when there were only sparse records of the Lifeboat. Jack laboured long and hard on this task in Record Offices, Libraries and from the memories of his friends.

It had always been his intention to continue with Part 2. However his many other interests involved him in much effort and advancing years did not help. Sadly, he died in 1993.

He left though, many meticulously written notes about lifeboat events and services which we have now brought together to make Part 2. We (SJ and WK), have continued his style but added appendices on the Coxswains and the Lifeboats. The Coxswains were stalwart men, and still are the backbone of the RNLI. In the days we are talking of, they were giants in every sense of the word with powerful physiques to man pulling and sailing boats, and with the mental capacity to cope with the terrible conditions often encountered on service calls.

We have ended this volume in 1924 to coincide with the retirement of Coxswain Swan. This was also about the time of the introduction of motor lifeboats to Lowestoft. The first was the *John and Mary Meiklam of Gladswood* in 1921. She was renamed *Agnes Cross* in 1922.

The photographs we have used are credited in the captions. We are especially grateful to the Port of Lowestoft Research Society for allowing us extensive use of their photographic collection.
The chart at Figure 1 was reproduced from Admiralty chart 1504 by permission of the Controller of Her Majesty's Stationery Office. © Crown Copyright.

Any errors or omissions that there may be are entirely ours, but we hope sincerely that this volume will stand as a fitting memorial to our late dear friend Jack.

SJ and WK

Figure 1.

Sandbanks off Lowestoft and Great Yarmouth

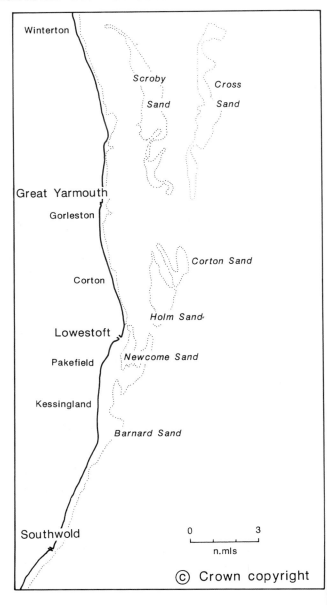

CHAPTER 1

Coxswain Hook 1877-1883

His Final Years

In 1876 the RNLI set about the task of replacing the ageing *Laetitia*. They went to the local yard of S Sparham where the old boat had been built back in 1850. The result was a Norfolk and Suffolk type boat very like the old one, 44ft x 12ft and rowing 14 oars. Since the inhabitants of Derby raised the money for her she was named after one of the MP's for Derby - Mr. Samuel Plimsoll. He performed the naming ceremony on 21 December 1876 at Sparham's yard on the North beach, and broke a bottle of wine on the stem.

Bob Hook took her out on her first service on 8 October 1877 to the brig **Hope** of Hartlepool with a cargo of deals and battens from Gothenburg to Poole. She had become leaky in a strong northerly gale, having earlier rescued the crew of a smack. The *Samuel Plimsoll* escorted her safely to Harwich since the prevailing weather made it impossible to get into Lowestoft.

On 10 November 1878 the Danish steamer **Gorm** grounded on the Holm Sand while bound from Riga to London with a cargo of oats. The *Samuel Plimsoll* under Hook took off the crew of 21. The steamer was later refloated and brought into the Roads by the harbour tugs. She left eventually for London in the tow of the tugs **Undaunted** and **Dreadnought**.

Later, on 27 November 1878 the *Samuel Plimsoll* was out again. The Colchester brig **Zosteria** with a cargo of railway iron was anchored in the north Roads in heavy weather. The cargo shifted and the crew hoisted a distress signal. The Lifeboat was towed out by the paddle tug **Despatch** and the crew of five were taken off. The next morning the tug got her off and towed her into the harbour. In December she was offered for sale by a local auctioneer, W T Balls who described her as "lying near the oil mills".

For the next two-and-a-half years there were no calls on the lifeboat, and only one in 1881. However 1882 was to make up for the calm with ten vessels being assisted in various ways from 28 October to 12 December when Hook carried out his last service.

At this time the Institution's rule regarding salvage was:

> "The Institution's boats will not as a general rule be employed to save property. When other aid is not to hand the crew may consider the Lifeboat loaned for that purpose. The owner of property saved will pay the crew, who will receive no reward from the Institution."

On 7 March 1882 the local smack LT436 **Alert** ran onto the outer edge of the Newcome Sand. The beachmen manned a yawl from the north beach but the seas were too heavy and they put back to get the lifeboat. The crew of the *Samuel Plimsoll*, on getting to the casualty, saw that the Pakefield boat *Two Sisters Mary and Hannah* had got there first and were towing the smack to harbour. For this the Pakefield boat received £105 in salvage less £10 for the Institution.

Both RNLI boats were administered by one Branch and the Chairman and Officers deprecated the fact that the beachmen launched a yawl first rather than the lifeboat, and in so doing lost the job. They recommended payment to the Lowestoft men of £8 16s the same as for a standard exercise launch. The Lowestoft beachmen refused the money which was eventually returned to the London HQ. Most beachmen thereafter considered themselves as having nothing to do with the Lifeboat.

The lack of proper payment for this service was to have serious repercussions in October that year on a day that was to become known as Black Saturday.

BLACK SATURDAY 28 October 1882

The week opened badly. On Tuesday 24 October, a fearful gale suddenly sprang up from the south-east, but fortunately shipping casualties were few. The schooner **Active** of Inverness while trying to make Yarmouth roads from Orfordness finished up on Corton beach. The crew were rescued by the rocket apparatus. She was towed off the next day by the tug **Despatch** and brought into Lowestoft harbour. Another Scottish schooner the **Adventure** of Montrose struck the Holm Sand early in the day. She was assisted off by beachmen who took her to Yarmouth roads for £25.

> "Scarcely had the furious hurricane of Tuesday, with its list of casualties not yet completed, passed away when we were visited with another storm which, if it did not quite rival its predecessor in violence, has been as far as shipping is concerned, much more prolific in disaster, and will for many a day and year be remembered as one of the most serious visitations of the kind this neighbourhood has ever experienced."

So a reporter in the *Lowestoft Journal* of 4 November 1882 started his description of Saturday the 28th and its events which, because of the tragic and unnecessary loss of life which occurred, has become known as "Black Saturday" to the people of Lowestoft.

Daylight that morning revealed a very bleak scene. Upwards of 200 vessels were anchored in the Roads between Yarmouth and Lowestoft, and the strong north-east wind put them on a perilous lee shore. Torrential rain made it at times difficult to see the shore for the crews to check if they were dragging. Some cables soon broke. Before 10 o'clock, three brigantines the **Anne**, the **Louisa** of Faversham and the **Polka** of Maldon, were assisted into Lowestoft having lost their anchors and chains. Other skippers, deciding that discretion was the better part, made their way to either Yarmouth or Lowestoft harbours.

During the morning, as the gale force winds continued to strengthen, the number of vessels running for Lowestoft increased and the tugs **Despatch** and **Rainbow** were kept busy answering calls for help. Because the harbour was already crowded with the Lowestoft and Scottish herring boats, the small tug **Imperial** was fully occupied moving vessels through the bridge into the inner harbour. Many of the lifeboat's crew and other beachmen were also hard at work assisting with mooring ropes, or at the pumps, or helping clear some of the damaged rigging and gear.

A few vessels which broke adrift in Yarmouth Roads managed to get their spare anchor ready, and anchor again in Corton Roads. Amongst them was the brig **Messenger** of Blyth with coal for Spain.

Onlookers on Ness Point about 2pm reported that they saw a procession of vessels coming along the Roads with distress flags in their rigging. This procession, they said, continued until after 4pm by which time the coastguards were reporting winds of force 12. From where the people stood they could also see the lifeboat house, and were more than a little surprised that there was no sign of the lifeboat or of any activity there.

Although a few of the earlier arrivals reported that they had touched bottom as they entered the harbour, it was not until low water at about 4.30pm that the trouble really started. The first casualty was the little schooner **Hope** of Rye bound from Hartlepool for Sidmouth, which had already lost three anchors. She grounded off the recently completed north extension. Beachmen were promptly on the scene, but before they could do anything, a large vessel without any anchors was seen approaching. This was the **Messenger** which had broken from her remaining anchor in Corton Roads. The inevitable collision was somehow avoided, to the cheers of the onlookers on the piers, and she just managed to miss the stranded schooner. Unfortunately she also missed the harbour entrance, and running down the side of the pier grounded near the reading room at about 5pm.

Not long after the **Messenger** had passed a large schooner appeared making for the harbour. She did not miss the **Hope**, and for a time the two vessels lay in the harbour mouth grinding against each other. Suddenly an extra strong gust of wind caught the larger vessel and literally lifted the smaller one off the ground, and they were both swept into the harbour. The large schooner was the **Hinderika Grietje Almina** of Emden, bound from Goole to Messina with coal. She was in the harbour alright, but then collided with a brig and received further damage.

By now, the coastguards under their Chief Officer Lt. George Symes, were on the South pier with their rocket apparatus to help the **Messenger**. Her Master, Peter Sorensen, declined to leave at first as he did not think there was much danger in what he thought was a sheltered position. No doubt some of the beachmen who were on board put him wise to the danger and he soon changed his mind. He and his crew of seven and seven beachmen were brought safely on to the pier.

The schooner **Alma** of Exeter was the next vessel to miss the harbour, finishing up on the south beach not far from the Royal Hotel, the coastguards bringing the Master and crew of five ashore.

The two tugs **Despatch** and **Rainbow** were to remain with steam up throughout that night since the Harbour Master was sure that the lifeboats would be calling for their help before the night was out. The **Rainbow** was berthed on the north side of the harbour ready for the brass tally from the Lowestoft lifeboat, while **Despatch** lay in the south basin handy for the Pakefield tally. These brass tallies, sent by the Coxswains of the lifeboats by any willing runner, were stamped 'LLB' for Lowestoft lifeboat and 'PLB' for the one from Pakefield.

A little ketch came slowly up the Roads, struggling against the strong tide, trying to make the safety of Lowestoft harbour. She was the **QED** of Dartmouth with coal for Clacton. Captain Warner had sailed from Hartlepool as soon as Tuesday's gale had blown itself out, and had hoped to make Clacton beach by the weekend. This fresh gale caught him a bad spot, and he was worried, particularly for his wife and three children who were on board. Having weathered Ness Point with difficulty he realised that he was not going to make the harbour, and seeing a crowd of men on shore near the gas works decided to run ashore there. Bob Hook and some of his men were in that crowd. They got hold of a rope floated ashore from the ship and got busy, rescuing Mrs Warner and her three children aged 6, 10 and 12 who were taken charge of by Mrs Hayward of Nelson Score East. The three crew were next, followed by the Captain and all were taken to the Sailors' Home in Commercial Road.

Bob Hook and the beachmen went home to change their wet clothes.

A short while after, Mr Henderson, the lifeboat Superintendent, told Lt. Symes that while the crew of the **QED** were safe he had received a telegram from Pakefield saying that there was a vessel ashore under Pakefield cliffs and the surf lifeboat could not reach her. The coastguards set off for Pakefield.

Five miles down the coast the coastguards at Kessingland had been watching the happenings at Lowestoft. Spotting a vessel heading for Pakefield beach, and assuming that the Lowestoft rocket apparatus was fully occupied they collected their gear and under Mr Charles Rashleigh set off for Pakefield.

The vessel which had gone ashore there was the brigantine **William Thrift** of Dundee with coal for London. Captain Raine had earlier slipped 80 fathoms of cable and his anchor to make for Lowestoft harbour intending to enter, but being unable to do without assistance, had prepared his spare anchor. He anchored off the harbour entrance and signalled for a tug, but before he was answered the cable parted and the vessel drove ashore on Pakefield beach.

During the afternoon Coxswain Warford of Pakefield No.1 boat had been watching events also and about mid-afternoon he thought it would be advisable to get their big boat the *Two Sisters Mary and Hannah* afloat. Remembering the row with the Secretary over permission to launch earlier in the year, he sent a messenger to the Secretary's house. Mr Warman was out. About an hour later, seeing the difficulties developing all around and the **William Thrift** heading for the shore with men in her rigging he decided to launch the surf lifeboat *Henry Burford RN* even though the Secretary had not returned. There was a fearful sea pounding on the beach, but they managed to get the boat afloat under Coxswain William Barber, before the brigantine actually beached. However, no matter how hard they tried, the lifeboat was driven back every time by the force of wind and tide. By now the Secretary had returned and consultations with Coxswain Warford led to the telegram being sent to Mr Henderson, which resulted in the arrival of the coastguards and their rocket apparatus.

Linesman Beebe threw his first shot true, the crew pulled the heavy line across to their ship and the breeches buoy was sent over and made fast. The crew of five were brought ashore and taken to the nearby Cliff Hotel in Pakefield Road, where Tom Hastings the proprietor took charge of them. As the hotel was shut for the winter and there were no staff, a kindly neighbour, Mr W F Larkins JP who lived in Holm View, two houses away, sent in some blankets, hot soup and a grouse pie.

Shortly afterwards the **William Thrift** went to pieces.

As the survivors were being refreshed another vessel was seen driving ashore a mile further south. Again the Lowestoft men recovered their gear, packed it up and got on the move, but a few yards away, as they turned into Pakefield Street, they met the Kessingland men. A quick consultation and the Kessingland men turned towards the new casualty. She was the **Seaham** of Faversham with coal for Portsmouth. Her Master, Captain Slater, and his five crew were all saved by breeches buoy.

6

The Lowestoft coastguards turned for home.

Even as Lt. Symes and his men had earlier set off up London Road to Pakefield, a great need of their services arose off the South beach again. Two brigs, the **Susanna Dixon** of Whitby and the **Mornington** of Colchester collided near the harbour entrance, and then stranded on a bank a few hundred yards south of the South pier, on the bottom of the tide.

In north-east gales, a series of sand banks, the Corton, Holm, and Newcome, which stretch along the coast a little way offshore, afford some degree of shelter at low tide. As the tide rises however, their influence decreases. Not long after the two brigs stranded the rising tide brought heavy rollers thundering across their decks. The **Susanna Dixon** nearest the South pier soon lost a mast, and her crew of seven took to their small boat and rowed over to the **Mornington**, where they joined the crew of eight already in the rigging.

Earlier on that Saturday morning the brig **Isis** of Cowes (Captain Souter) with coal from Hartlepool for the Isle of Wight brought up in Yarmouth Roads. For some hours she rode easily at anchor, but during the afternoon first the port chain broke and then the starboard one so that by six o'clock she was adrift. The Captain decided to make for Lowestoft, but knew that with a draught of 13ft 3inches he would not be able to enter at that state of the tide. However he thought Lowestoft a better place for saving life. Arriving off the harbour entrance he steered to pass outside the South pier, but a dragging starboard chain made the vessel almost unmanagable. She crashed, first into the pier head, and then drove down along the bank into the half submerged **Susanna Dixon**. The two vessels lay close together hammering into the sands and each other, the crew of the **Isis** clinging desperately to the mainmast rigging. She soon started to break up, the mainmast, and men, falling across the small ship's boat on the deck. Some crew were still clinging to the mast when it was swept overboard sometime after 9 o'clock. Shortly before this happened, the Captain had put his one and only lifebelt on the youngest member of the crew, 16 year old William Meen. When he was washed over with the mast, thanks to the lifebelt he was able to struggle to the South pier, where he was thrown a rope, hauled to safety and taken to the Harbour Inn. He later joined many other survivors at the Sailors' Home in Commercial Road.

Having done all he could for young Meen, Captain Souter went into the rigging of the foremast where he was joined by the mate Frederick Churchill, the remaining four of the crew going overboard about the same time as

Meen. One of them George Churchill was a strong swimmer, and struck out for the nearby **Susanna Dixon**, but finding her in a worse state than the **Isis**, he went for the shore. Staying calm and letting the waves help him he made for the dark hulk of a vessel he could see near the shore. He managed to get aboard. She was the **Alma** from which the coastguards had taken the crew just before going to Pakefield. The three other crew members, George Greenfield, Thomas Barton and William Carpenter were lost, Greenfield's body washing ashore on the North beach a few days later.

The heavy rain which had persisted all day gave way and breaks in the storm clouds allowed the moon to illuminate the terrifying scene. The **Mornington** had settled down, and only her masts were showing, with fifteen men still clinging to them. On the nearby **Isis**, the two survivors of her crew could be seen in the rigging of the foremast. Of the **Susanna Dixon** there was no sign.

On the South pier, William Hazard, a solicitor from Harleston, had been watching the scene for some time. Any minute now, he thought, the lifeboat would come on the scene and he would be able to witness the daring rescue of the poor souls on the wrecks. Time passed and no sign of the lifeboat, he became puzzled and asked some of the bystanders where the boat could be. Several men told him that there was trouble with the crew over payment for a previous launch, and one surly beachman retorted "Let those who rob the crew save the lives." Thoroughly disturbed now, Hazard accepted the offer by a man to take him to the lifeboat house, while another man, John Ambler, a seaman turned dairyman offered to go and ask Hook to meet the party at the boatshed. Arriving at the shed, Hazard found a few seamen there, but the shed was locked. He was joined there by Ambler, who reported that Hook refused to come, or let the lifeboat be launched.

Later, when giving evidence at the Board of Trade Inquiry in December, Hazard said he went to Hook's place, the Fishermen's Arms Tavern, in Christchurch Square, at about 7.30pm, and found him in his shirt sleeves smoking a pipe. (Hook said later that he had just changed after rescuing the crew of the **QED**). Hazard told Hook of the state of things off the South pier, of the men in ships' rigging, and urged him to get the boat out and do his job. Hook again said that the boat would not go out. Really angry now, the solicitor said to Hook "The poor fellows are drowning. It is nothing but absolute murder. You might as well stick a knife into them as serve them as you are." Hazard returned to the boat shed where he found more men had gathered. He told them that if it was a question of money, he would give £1 to every man who went out in the boat, and a Mr Stacey promised a further £1 each. Just then Hook appeared on the scene, and after a bit more argument, opened up the boat shed doors. From that moment on, he did all he could towards getting the boat out and into the water.

It was now after 8 o'clock. If the boat had been on the beach and the hauling off warp in position, as they were supposed to have been since October 1st, they could have launched in about 15 minutes. As it was, however, the boat was still in the shed, and she had to be dragged about 500 feet over a soft undulating beach, in the dark, by men who were not used to handling the heavy 10 ton boat. At times they were too eager and dragged the boat off the skids. Once or twice the ropes broke under the strain and sent men sprawling. Also, with the little ketch **QED** right in line of launch, the turn skid was needed to slew the boat, and it could not be found. Neither could Bob Hook. He had gone off to help the crew of the brigantine **Launceston** which had just come ashore inside the recently completed extension to the North pier. The crew had got into their small boat, but had great difficulty in landing through the surf. Walter Stock, a local smack owner went boldly into the surf, sometimes nearly up to his neck, and helped several of the crew. He was only kept from being swept away by other men hanging onto his coat tails. (Payment for the launch to his smack **Alert** in March was the cause of the present crew trouble).

About the same time another vessel ran ashore on the South beach. She was the brig **Prosper** of Carnarvon. She managed to miss the other vessels on the bank, and thanks to the higher tide, and the assistance of heavy breakers, she landed well up the beach, south of the **Alma**. The crew managed to float a line ashore attached to a barrel. A heavier line was hauled after it, and four of the crew came ashore along it. They had to leave on board an old man suffering from rheumatism. On learning of this, James Hall, Master of the fishing boat **Trial** went up the rope, made a sling into which he put the old man, and then pushed him down the rope to willing hands on the beach. (Hall later received the RNLI Silver medal and £2 for this brave deed.)

Earlier in the afternoon further north, the Whitby brig **Runo** broke adrift from her anchors in Yarmouth Roads, and collided with another Whitby ship **Warrior Queen**. Both were so badly damaged that they had to be abandoned. The crew of five from **Runo** were fortunate and made a good landing at Lowestoft at about 7pm. The crew of eight from the **Warrior Queen** were unfortunate - very unfortunate. When they got into their boat they found no rowlocks and only a few oars, they could not go back aboard because it was too dangerous. So they had to make do. They ran before the wind and fashioned rowlocks out of the floorboards, but they were very poor and broke rapidly. Seas were running so high that they were lucky not to be swamped and as darkness fell they lost sight of land. After eight interminable hours the Captain sighted the lights of Southwold and they started to row ashore. While doing so the rowlocks on the starboard side gave way, causing the boat to swing broadside to the heavy seas which promptly capsized her. Only a Swedish seaman survived; Charles Abson managed to reach the beach, coming ashore at Walberswick. He was able to walk as far as the house of a fisherman, William Cross, who helped him to the Blue Anchor where he was well looked after by the landlady Mrs Veasey and her neighbours.

About 8.30pm, at the height of the gale and unseen from Lowestoft, the ss **Secret** went onto the Newcome Sands. This was the end of a voyage which she should never have started. Leaving Shields for Plymouth on October 14th, Robinson Bell the boatswain at the time, said she steamed south in fair weather, but with a head wind, and made about two knots. When the tide turned she went backwards. Her three lifeboats were all warped, and all her decks opened, and the pumps were choked. What sails she had, he said, were like pieces of brown paper. She put into Hartlepool, after a journey of nine hours for 22 miles. Here Bell refused to go further and left.

The **Secret** eventually reached Corton Roads about 4.30pm on Saturday, and anchored there because she could not make progress against the tide. At about 8.15pm she broke from her anchor and drifted onto the Newcombe. Flares were shown, but were unanswered. The port lifeboat was lowered, but was stove in, the jolly boat was smashed, so only the starboard boat was left. This was lowered but started to fill. Some of the crew got in and began bailing but water came in faster, and they decided to get back onto the **Secret**. Before the last man, Joseph McCarthy could do so however, the rope broke and the boat drifted away and capsized. McCarthy siezed an oar and clutching this he drifted ashore at Kessingland. Here he was found by Mr Knights who, with his wife did all they could for him. He later came to the Sailors' Home in Lowestoft. The **Secret** became a complete wreck and the remainder of the crew were lost.

Along the coast at Corton, several vessels were lost with their crews during the evening. A schooner drove on the breakwater at the north end of Colman's property. The coastguards fired a line across her, but it was found that the vessel had already been abandoned. This must have been the schooner which collided with the **Evening Star** of Hull which was anchored in Corton Roads, and which, as a result of the collision lost her bowsprit and mainmast. The unknown then continued on her way, narrowly missing a vessel called **Zenobia**, and driving on the beach where she broke up. Another unknown schooner came ashore just to the south of the Colman land. The first line thrown landed too high in the rigging and a second was fired. This landed across the forecastle, but before the crew could get it, the vessel broke in two and she went to pieces.

Back on the North beach, the launchers were still struggling with the lifeboat. Hook, before he went off to the **Launceston**, left instructions for the boat to be taken to the south of the **QED**, but some who thought they knew better started to work her to the north. They found Hook was right and valuable time was lost. So it was not until about 11.30pm that the *Samuel Plimsoll* was finally launched.

Around 10pm it was estimated that there were between 3000 and 4000 people gathered on the piers and South beach. Disgusted by the continued absence of the lifeboat, six local fishermen, John Dale, William Herrod, Frederick Hall, Edward Sharman, William Wilson and Theophilus Young put out in a small boat to try to rescue some of the dispairing men in the rigging of the stranded ships. They made their way out of the harbour to cheers from the onlookers. It was not long however, before they found themselves in trouble. The strong tidal current near the pier heads was sweeping them inshore of the brigs they wanted to reach. As they struggled, one by one the rowlocks broke, and they were carried well past the very men they set out to help. Eventually their shouts for help were heard on board the schooner **Merton** anchored off Kirkley. A rope was thrown and the six men taken off, the empty boat drifting away in the night.

Some 45 minutes dragged by. Suddenly cheers were heard near the pier entrance. The coastguards had arrived back from Pakefield. The rocket apparatus was quickly set up, and George Beebe, aiming for the foremast of the **Isis**, once again got his first shot onto the target. It was mentioned later at one of the enquiries, that chief boatman Beebe "during the whole evening never had occasion to throw a line more than once, as he threw them so true." After some trouble a block and whip line were hauled to the vessel, made fast, and the breeches-buoy sent out. The Mate, Frederick Churchill, was first to come from the wreck. As he neared the pier it was seen that he was in trouble - instead of being in the buoy he was hanging onto it and was nearly finished. Coastguard Charles Child jumped into the sea and swam out to meet the man at great risk to his own life. He helped him to the side of the pier, and waited while Churchill was hauled to safety. During this time he was battered against the timber piling despite his efforts to keep clear. By the time he was hauled out he was so bruised that he had to be assisted home. (He later received the Board of Trade Bronze medal and £2 for his act of bravery).

Before the buoy could be sent back to the **Isis**, a further burst of cheering was heard from the pier head announcing the arrival of the lifeboat - at long last. Working his way through the tangle of wreckage alongside the **Isis**, Hook picked up Captain Souter. Passing the clean swept **Susanna Dixon** he took the *Samuel Plimsoll* as near as he could to the **Mornington**, where he took on board her crew of eight, and the seven from the **Susanna Dixon**. These 16, more than half dead from cold and fatigue were landed at the Bridge steps, and immediately taken to the Sailors' Home nearby.

Although the lifeboat had completed the work on the brigs which the coastguards had started the coastguards had more to do. A cry for help was heard from the **Alma** from which they had already saved the crew. They found there George Churchill who had swum over from the **Isis** earlier. He was soon brought ashore and reunited with his shipmates in the warmth of the Sailors' Home.

A three-masted schooner **Anna** of Boulogne with pitch and tar from Archangel for Bristol, was lost off Corton sometime during the night. The beaches at Hopton and Corton were soon strewn with casks and barrels from her cargo. It is believed also that a Danish vessel was lost in the same area, while out in the Roads the **Ryhope** of Hartlepool foundered. The crew of six took to their boat, but it capsized and three of them were swept away by heavy seas. The Master, William Booth and two of the crew managed to cling to the upturned boat. Their shouts were heard on board the steamer **Stanton** of Goole, and they were picked up and taken to Greenwich.

The last known casualty of this terrible night occurred in the early hours of Sunday morning. The brigantine **Sovereign** of Colchester with coal for Portsmouth from Seaham parted from her anchors at about 5am in Corton Roads and drifted onto the Newcome Sands. The crew took to the boat and made harbour safely.

The gale blew itself out during the night, and Sunday morning dawned fine and clear. The tugs were out at first light, as several ships had flags in their rigging. One of the first to be assisted in was the **Merton**, on board of which George Dale and his five companions had been glad to take refuge the previous night, after their lifesaving efforts had gone wrong. The **Merton** had had a bad trip, losing several sails and her main-topmast in a gale off the

Humber on the 24th. She arrived off Lowestoft late on the 27th and anchored under the Holm Sand. When trying to recover her anchor on Saturday afternoon, the chain parted. She re-anchored off Kirkley about 5pm. On Sunday morning at about 5am this anchor parted. As his crew were weary after their rough passage, Captain Gifford asked Dale and his men if they could help get sail on the vessel, and he also asked Dale if, with his local knowledge, he could keep the vessel clear of the Newcome Sand. This Dale did, working the vessel almost as far as Kessingland. Here they were picked up by the tug **Despatch** which received £40 for towing them into Lowestoft. Dale then put in a claim for salvage, maintaining that he and his men had saved the vessel, which, with cargo was valued at £200. After a court hearing, Dale was offered, and accepted, £10 10s.

Just over a fortnight later it was reported in several local papers that Lady Stracey of The Hall, Rackheath, had sent to Dale and each of his five companions

> "...a splendid quarto Bible, handsomely bound with clasp and gilt edges, containing also a register for births, marriages and deaths. On the flyleaf the inscription -

> > 'A small token from Lady Stracey, with admiration for his bravery on the night of October 28th 1882' ."

After the wild happenings of the Saturday night, many of the inhabitants of the town came at daylight to a scene of tragic death and destruction. On the North beach were the hulks of the little ketch **QED** and the brigantine **Launceston**. The brig **Messenger** was firmly bedded alongside the South pier, while the schooner **Alma** and the brig **Prosper** were high and dry on the South beach. On the bank, a hundred yards or so offshore, was the brig **Mornington**, both masts still standing, and nearby the battered remains of the other two brigs, **Susanna Dixon** and **Isis**. Well out on the Newcome Sands could be seen the masts of the brigantine **Sovereign**, and the remains of the steamer **Secret**. Along the beach at Pakefield was the hull of the brigantine **William Thrift**, and nearer Kessingland the remains of the schooner **Seaham**. Having picked their way through the broken timbers, spars and other wreckage on the beach, the spectator was then free to have a look at the more fortunate casualties, those which had made the safety of the South basin and Inner harbour.

The gale might be over, but there were signs of a storm brewing ashore.

Much public disquiet was generated by the happenings of "Black Saturday" and several meetings were held and resolutions passed.

The Churchwardens of Lowestoft convened a public meeting on Tuesday 31 October at the Skating Rink (now the site of the Marina Theatre). This meeting was "largely attended" and seems to have drawn contrasts between the efficient saving of life by the Coastguards with their rocket apparatus and the tardy launching of the lifeboat. It was unanimously resolved that:

> "The National Lifeboat Institution be respectfully requested to hold a Public Enquiry at Lowestoft, relative to the cause of the lamentable delay in launching of the Lowestoft Lifeboat on Saturday last and also the cause of the Pakefield Lifeboat not having been launched on that occasion."

A second resolution was passed after the main business had been concluded:

> "The Directors of the Great Eastern Railway Coy., be respectfully memorialised to institute a Public Enquiry with regard to the neglect of the use of their steam tugs at Lowestoft for the purpose of saving life on Saturday last."

Apparently the meeting felt that the tugs had been primarily used for salvage and gaining salvage payments.

In the severe weather conditions of that night it would have been an act of folly for a paddle driven steam tug to attempt to get near wrecked vessels, surrounded as they would be with floating masts, spars and rigging, for the purpose of rescuing people. The paddles would have been smashed and the tug very likely would have become a casualty herself.

On 2 November a meeting of the RNLI Committee in London noted the fact that "the crew of the Lowestoft lifeboat declined for some hours to man their boat." They determined to hold the most searching enquiry and appointed two of their District Lifeboat Inspectors, Capt. Chetwynd RN and Cmdr. Nepean RN, to assist the local Committee in their investigations.

At the same time as the London meeting was deliberating, a special meeting of the Lowestoft and Pakefield Branch of the RNLI was being held in the Court House. George Edwards Esq, Chairman of the Committee was in the chair. Also present were Messrs J Peto JP, W F Larkins JP, B Preston, W Warman (Hon. Sec. for Pakefield), W R Massingham (Harbour Master),

J Henderson (Lifeboat Supt.), F Morse (Branch Hon. Sec), the Rev. J F Reeve BA JP, and the Rev. C J Steward MA. Reference was made to the launch to the **Alert** on 7 March and to the Lowestoft Committee's recommending a payment for a practise launch (4/- per man) instead of for a night service (£1 per man). Similar instances were reported where the crew got the correct payments. There were also references to other cases of crew misconduct.

Hook informed the Committee that he wished to resign his position saying, "I have had nearly 30 years of it, and no one would believe what I have had to put up with." There was further heated discussion as to why the Lifeboat was not on the beach as ordered, and why Pakefield No.1 boat was not launched.

That same evening a meeting was held at the Great Eastern Hotel in Denmark Road, to consider the establishment of a volunteer lifeboat. It was proposed by H G Jones and W Stock, both smack owners, that an appeal be circulated immediately with a copy being sent to the Directors of The Great Eastern Railway Coy. In view of the fact that the boat was eventually obtained and was called *Carolina Hamilton* after the wife of the Chairman of the GER Lord Claude Hamilton, it seems likely that more than a little help came from the company.

A further resolution was also carried unanimously:

> "That a few gentlemen meet immediately after this meeting for the
> purpose of protecting the   fame of our Lowestoft beachmen, also
> for obtaining a full enquiry into the management of the local
> Committee of the National Lifeboat Institution as at present carried
> on."

Adam Adams (Improvement Commissioner and grocer) and J S Sterry (ship owner and coal merchant) were selected to lead the attack, and after discussion, a list of questions which would require answering was drawn up.

The Public Enquiry opened at the Skating Rink on Friday 3 November. The local Committee was there in full, augmented by Messrs FS Worthington (surgeon), J Rounce (Lloyds Agent), W Youngman (Churchwarden, Improvement Commissioner and bank manager), J L Clemence (architect and surveyor) and A Stebbings (stationer and publisher of the *Lowestoft Journal*). Adam Adams opened the proceedings by questioning the local Committee about their jobs. The Chairman George Edwards said he was nearly 80 years old and lived at Carlton Colville (3 miles west of Lowestoft) and did not think he should need to go to the beach to see if the Committee's orders were being carried out. He offered to resign if someone who had spent more money and time for Lowestoft Lifeboat could be found. Frederick Morse the Honorary Secretary lived at Ipswich. He felt it was only his duty to write up the records of what transpired in the running of the station. He did not think that he had to have anything to do with the actual station. That was the job of John Henderson the Lifeboat Superintendent who managed the station and the Coxswain who looked after the boat. The second day was taken up with trying to find out what happened and when. On the Monday following a number of beachmen were questioned at length. The Enquiry was then closed by Capt. Chetwynd.

On Monday 13 November the findings were made public. The enquiry found that:

- The Hon Secretary Mr Morse has erred through misconception of the duties and responsibilities of his office, with the result that a very important portion of his duties has been omitted.
- Mr Henderson, the Hon. Supt. of the lifeboat has unpardonably and unaccountably neglected his duties to the most serious detriment of the efficiency of the station, and the more particularly on this disasterous occasion.
- Robert Hook the Coxswain deserves the severest censure for the gross and wilful neglect of his duties. This is the more to be regretted coming as it does after a series of excellent and gallant services performed over a period of nearly 30 years, and for which he has twice received the Institution's Silver medal.
- The Beach Companies, in view of the circumstances attending their services to the **Alert** on 7 March had reasonable cause for dissatisfaction and complaint, and the course they adopted of having nothing more to do with the lifeboat was within their rights.
- Pakefield No.1 boat was not launched in consequence of a most lamentable misunderstanding on the part of the Coxswain George Warford of the meaning of the orders given him by Mr Warman the Honorary Secretary.

One result of the enquiry was that on 24 November a payment for the launch to the **Alert** on 7 March was again sent down to the crew. This time however, it was the full scale for a night service - £1 per man.

The second enquiry called for on 31 October into the conduct of the GER tugs was never held. The resolution was sent to the Directors of the GER, who replied saying that they saw no fault with the Company or its servants.

The *Ipswich Journal* of Saturday 18 November 1882 reported:

> "On Tuesday morning the lifeboatmen of Lowestoft retrieved their character by making an efficient rescue from a stranded vessel."

On Monday night 13 November a tremendous easterly gale blew resulting in a number of vessels in trouble in the Roads. Further out the Norwegian barque **Berthon** was making her way south down the North Sea. By Tuesday morning the Master saw what he took to be the **Shipwash** lightvessel realising only too late that it was the **Corton** lightvessel. He let go both anchors, but the way on the vessel parted them and she ran onto the outer part of the Holm Sand at 8.45am. Her plight was seen by the beachmen and the crew were called.

Following a previous launch the lifeboat was afloat in the harbour, but she was having crew trouble again, this time because too many eager beachmen got on board. Eventually she was towed out with a crew of 25, six more than normal, but only after the small harbour tug was sent out to the Roads to recall the bigger tug. Hook took the *Samuel Plimsoll* across the Holm Sand to the ship and successfully rescued her crew of eight.

Later the same day the *Samuel Plimsoll* was out to two vessels both in trouble in the Roads. The brigantine **Wilhelmina** and the brig **Harkaway** were towed in by the tugs with the lifeboat standing by.

For the **Berthon** service the Institution sent down 10/- per man for the authorised crew of 19, 30/- for the steam tug and £5 for the crew of the harbour tug **Imperial** in recognition of "the small harbour launch going out in heavy seas in a gale to recall the tugs." No doubt £1 each soothed the mens' feelings after having their tug described as a launch! On the evening after the rescue a meeting was held at the Harbour Hotel at which the sum of £27 8s.2d was raised and presented to Coxswain Hook for the crew.

On 22 November the Rev. T A Nash, Rector of Lowestoft, chaired a meeting attended by the full lifeboat crew, Capt. Porter Master of **Despatch** and Capt.Massingham Harbour Master. Mr Nash spoke of the bravery of the lifeboat crew saying that some recognition of it was called for. Mr Frank Seago had organised a collection of funds for the medals which were presented to the lifeboat crew and the two Captains. They were of a Maltese Cross design and inscribed:

"The crew of the **Berthon** rescued Nov. 14th 1882."

On the reverse was the name of the man to whom it was presented. The supplier was Mr E F Craike who donated the morocco leather and silk lined cases.

So, in a period of three weeks the Lowestoft beachmen had been reviled as cowards and given medals for their bravery. Their troubles were not over yet, however.

Because of the loss of life which occurred on 28 October, the Board of Trade held an enquiry. This opened at the Public Hall, London Road, Lowestoft on 7 December. There was a Wreck Commissioner, four Nautical Assessors and various barristers. Unable to enquire into all the losses on that dreadful night, the Board decided to investigate three of them. The brig **Isis** from which three men were lost, the brigantine **William Thrift** whose crew were all saved by the coastguards and the ss **Secret** from which 12 out of 13 were lost.

In the cases of the **Isis** and the **William Thrift**, the Court could find no fault with the gear supplied to the vessels, nor with the actions of the Officers and crew. Five days were then spent enquiring into the details of the steamer **Secret**. The Commissioner found that the vessel was in an utterly unfit and unseaworthy condition when she set out from Shields, defective in hull, equipment and machinery, and overloaded. T H Williams, her owner, was to blame for the loss, and was ordered to pay £200 towards the costs. The Court then enquired deeply into why assistance was not promptly rendered by the lifeboat and found that:

- Signals of distress were not attended to owing to the unhappy dispute about payment
- The local Committee were to blame in not awarding £1 for a night service by the lifeboat to the **Alert**; that Mr Morse and Mr Henderson had divided the duties of secretary and superintendent between them, and the latter had not seen Capt. Nepean's instruction carried out nor reported the lapse to the Committee. The Court, however, did not forget that Mr Henderson had domestic afflictions at his house (his wife was dying)
- The conduct of Hook was very bad indeed

- The crew of the lifeboat had behaved in a disgraceful manner
- The Court had every reason to believe that Warford, the Pakefield Coxswain was intent upon his duty, but that there were unhappy misapprehensions on his part on the meaning of Mr Warman's instructions
- Nobody on that station was to blame regarding Mr Warman's giving directions in a temper and Mr Warford obeying them in such circumstances
- Signals are not in use at Lowestoft or Pakefield, but it is desirable that they should be.   (referring to assembly signals for calling out the crew)

The Annual meeting of subscribers to the Lowestoft and Pakefield Branch of the RNLI was held in the Police Court on 17 January 1883. Several resignations were tendered: Mr George Edwards, Chairman; Mr Frederick Morse, Secretary; Mr Warman the Pakefield Secretary, Mr W F Larkins, Mr Henderson and Bob Hook. Mr B Preston was elected Secretary with powers of launching passed to the Coxswain of the boat. Mr Dance was elected assistant secretary to supervise efficiency of boat and gear. The Rev Lewis Price accepted the post of Hon. Secretary of the Pakefield boats.

The new Coxswain of the Lowestoft boat was William Jenner Capps and the 2nd Coxswain Daniel Ayers.

So, Coxswain Hook retired after many years of faithful service, marred only by the unfortunate events of the year before. During his time as Coxswain he had saved 315 lives; 159 in the *Victoria*, 92 in the same boat renamed *Laetitia* and finally 64 in the *Samuel Plimsoll*.

The saving of these people must stand as a fitting tribute to one of the 'characters' of 19th century Lowestoft.

Table 1

Services under Coxswain Hook 1877-1882

1877 *Samuel Plimsoll*
8 Oct	brig, **Hope** of Hartlepool, Holm	escorted
7 Nov	lugger, **Pet** (LT132), Newcome	saved 11 + dog

1878 *Samuel Plimsoll*
10 Nov	ss **Gorm** of Copenhagen, Holm	saved 21
? Nov	**Harry and Ernest**	ns
27 Nov	brig, **Zosteria** of Colchester, N Roads	saved 5

1881 *Samuel Plimsoll*
3 Mar	smack, **Progress** of Lowestoft	ns

1882 *Samuel Plimsoll*
7 Mar	smack, **Alert** (LT436), Newcome	ns
28 Oct	brig, **Mornington** of Colchester, S Beach	saved 8
	brig, **Susanna Dixon** of Whitby, S Beach	saved 8
	brig, **Isis** of Cowes, S Beach	saved 1
29 Oct	ketch, **Evening Star** of Hull, Corton	stood by
13 Nov	**Maraquita**	ns
14 Nov	barque, **Berthon** of Norway, Holm	saved 8
	brig't, **Wilhelmina** of Exeter, S Roads	assisted
	brig, **Harkaway** of Shoreham, S Roads	assisted
15 Nov	schooner, **Jane** of Faversham, S Roads	landed 2
18 Nov	barque, **Nimrod** of Liverpool, Holm	ns
12 Dec	unknown steamer, Corton	ns

Coxswain Robert Hook, he was in charge of the
Lowestoft lifeboats from 1853 until 1883.
(*W Keith Collection*)

RNLB *Samuel Plimsoll* (ON22), stationed at Lowestoft from 1867 until 1905. She is shown here at her moorings in Lowestoft harbour.

(*J W Mitchley Collection*)

The schooner **Alma** of Exeter and brig **Mornington** of Colchester (background) on Lowestoft South beach on 29 October 1882, the day following "Black Saturday".

(*PLRS Collection*)

The schooner **Alma** of Exeter and brig **Prosper** of
Carnarvon (background) on Lowestoft South beach on
29 October 1882, the day following "Black Saturday".
(*PLRS Collection*)

The private lifeboat *Carolina Hamilton* which was stationed at Lowestoft from 1883 until 1893.

(*PLRS Collection*)

The privately subscribed for medal presented to each crew member taking part in the rescue of the crew of the Norwegian barque **Berthon** on 14 November 1882.

(*PLRS Collection*)

CHAPTER 2

Coxswain Capps 1883 - 1901

The end of the 19th Century

Although William Capps was not officially appointed Coxswain until 17 January 1883, he was in charge of the boat when she went out on 9 January to the Goole ketches **Wonderful** and **John and Mary**. The tug which towed the *Samuel Plimsoll* out towed the two vessels in with the lifeboat standing by.

The *Eastern Daily Press* of 8 March 1883 reported "The schooner **Janie** (sic) of Runcorn was assisted into harbour by the lifeboat and a harbour tug." This bald statement concealed a rather unusual incident. On 6 March, the private lifeboat at California (Scratby) the *Royal Albert*, which was stationed about six miles north of Great Yarmouth, launched to the assistance of a ship which she saw safely as far as Southwold. The lifeboat then returned to Lowestoft where she was left in the charge of one of the crew while the others went home. In the days before motor boats this would have been a usual practice when the boat had gone so far from her station or the weather prevented return. Later in the evening flares were shown by the schooner **Jeannie** of Runcorn with coal for Plymouth. The beachmen found their lifeboat was inaccessible; the highest tides for 45 years having washed her off the skids and onto her side. The Pakefield No.1 boat was also out of service. Remembering that the California boat was afloat in the harbour and was similar to the *Samuel Plimsoll*, they borrowed it and went out. One report suggests they towed the **Jeannie** into harbour, however a few days later when the claim for salvage was adjudicated the lifeboat was awarded £30 and a tug £25 for towage and £15 for a broken towing rope. It is not recorded how much went to the California crew when they came to sail their boat home a few days later.

For the next three years the launches were mainly "assisted" or "no service", but in the autumn of 1886 William Capps had to launch to two of the new steam colliers.

On Friday 10 September 1886 two colliers, owned by Stephenson Clarke of London, were approaching Lowestoft. The 805 ton **Erasmus Wilson** was southbound to London with coal and passengers, while the 982 ton **Lord Alfred Paget** was bound to Jarrow with one passenger. Entering the Stanford Channel, Captain Bond of the **Erasmus Wilson** went to starboard to clear the channel buoy. Coming in the opposite direction the **Lord Alfred Paget** overtook a fishing boat and so the Captain had to port his helm. A stiff breeze had whipped up a heavy sea which added to the difficulties of navigation between the sandbanks, and a collision resulted. The laden **Erasmus Wilson** received a large gash abreast the foremast and began to fill. To prevent her sinking the Captain ran her on the South beach. The *Samuel Plimsoll* was towed out by the railway tug **Rainbow** and took off the men left on the **Wilson** - some had jumped onto the **Paget** when the collision took place. The lifeboat then took off these men also and landed them all at the old Trawl Market steps from where they were taken to the Sailors' Home in Commercial Road. In total 27 - 17 crew and 9 passengers from the **Wilson** and the solitary passenger from the **Paget** who decided to continue by rail it being safer!

D S Overy were awarded the salvage contract and began work on the Saturday, caulking and patching the gash in the side of the ship, whilst the beachmen began dumping some of the cargo of coal overboard. On the high tide of Sunday night the tugs **Rainbow** and **Despatch** towed the casualty off and into the harbour. Here temporary repairs to make the vessel seaworthy were completed and she sailed for London on Tuesday 21 September with some of Overy's men still on board. Permanent repairs were carried out in a dry dock in London. A few days later D S Overy received a letter from the London Salvage Association:

> "To certify that the ss **Erasmus Wilson** of London, 805 tons gross measurement after collision with the **Lord Alfred Paget** on the 10th inst., was beached at Lowestoft with a hole in the starboard bow 7 feet wide cutting through 11 planks of the deck and extending 12 feet down to the turn of the bilge, and with the assistance of Messrs D S Overy and Sons, shipwrights of Lowestoft, floated in two days and taken into Lowestoft harbour for temporary repairs which were completed in eight more when the steamer left for London arriving on the following day and dry docked for permanent repairs.

I have much pleasure in certfying as to the abilities and resources of D S Overy in such cases of emergency and salvage operations, and find them very intelligent people and capital workmen.

(Signed) Wm Richards RNR

Officer of The London Salvage Association."

The **Erasmus Wilson** continued under various owners and flags, and finally sank, after another collision, this time far away in Japanese waters on 12 June 1927.

In 1886 the large Pakefield lifeboat *Two Sisters Mary and Hannah* was moved to Lowestoft and became their No.2 until problems concerning the Pakefield boat sheds were sorted out. Launches continued to follow the pattern of "no service", including a launch to a ship reported to be on fire which turned out to be a bonfire on the beach (it was 5 November 1888!). A number of vessels were also "assisted".

A real business call came on 7 October 1889 when the *Two Sisters Mary and Hannah* launched to the three-masted schooner **Lymington** aground on the Holm Sand. She was bound from Sunderland with coal for Southampton. The lifeboat was afloat in the harbour and was ready in 10 minutes for the tug **Despatch** to tow her out into the Stanford Channel where the tow was cast off, the boat setting off across the sands to the casualty. The seas were very bad, and three extra big ones struck the lifeboat completely submerging her and washing one of the crew, Billy Capps, out of the boat. He was quickly hauled back, and the crew of six from the casualty were taken from the rigging. The lifeboat recrossed the sands safely this time and was taken in tow by the **Despatch**, reaching harbour just over an hour after leaving.

By 1890 new sites had been found for the two Pakefield boat sheds, and in March of that year the *Two Sisters Mary and Hannah* went home. Her place as the Lowestoft No.2 was taken by a new boat *The Stock Exchange* which had just been completed by W T Ellis in his yard on the North beach.

The first service launch of the new boat was on 19 July 1890 when two Yarmouth shrimpers **Don't Know** and **Edith and Alice** were brought up in Corton Roads. There was a strong north-east wind and a heavy sea running. The lifeboat was towed out by the GER tug **Imperial** with the tug **Rainbow** towing out the private lifeboat *Carolina Hamilton*. The Official lifeboat saved one man from each and both boats were towed to Lowestoft. The crew of *The Stock Exchange* reported that she "behaved splendidly".

Later, in early December, both *The Stock Exchange* and the Yarmouth lifeboat *Abraham Thomas* went to the scene of the wrecking of the collier **Hannah** on the Holm Sand. The vessel had disappeared before either boat got there and it was only wreckage which showed her name. The *Lowestoft Weekly Press* of 3 January 1891 reported that a Public Enquiry was held on 29 December 1890 concerning the loss of the **Hannah**. The Meeting was held with Sir Edward Birkbeck Bt. MP (Chairman RNLI) present and found that no blame attached to the lifeboat crews in any way.

The last three months of 1891 resulted in a flurry of calls to both the *Samuel Plimsoll* and *The Stock Exchange*. A particularly sad loss of sailors' lives occurred on 11 November. The *Samuel Plimsoll*, in tow of a tug, was only half a mile away when the lugger **Paramount** struck the Holm sand and capsized. The Master, James Davidson, told that he entered the Stanford Channel with heavily reefed canvas running before the gale. A large sea broke over the stern near the SW Holm buoy followed closely by a second. The boat was pushed onto the bank and the crew of six washed out of her. Three men managed to get hold of the capsized vessel's keel, but only two could hang on long enough for the lifeboat to get to them.

The Lifeboat Trials

During 1891 the RNLI arranged to hold trials of different types of Lifeboats. The boats were to be launched from a steep beach through surf, then beat to an outlying shoal, return and land on the steep beach, be hauled up and prepared for service. There were also to be trials from a flat beach. Because it possessed more of the necessary conditions than any place on the coast, Lowestoft was chosen as the venue. The North beach provided the steep shelving site, while the Children's Corner on the South beach just fitted the flat beach requirements. These trials, which were scheduled for February 1892, were advertised far and wide to encourage competition, but there was not a single entry to compete against established boats already in use.

The boats entered were:

- The new Lowestoft boat *The Stock Exchange* a Norfolk and Suffolk class, non-self-righting.
- A new 44ft self-righter built by Woolfe of Shadwell and crewed by men from Deal.

24

- A specially built boat designed by Mr Watson, Naval Architect to the RNLI, built by Henderson of Glasgow on the lines of one recently supplied to Southport.
- A tubular lifeboat, the ***Henry Richardson,*** from New Brighton.

Various serving and former Coxswains were chosen to sail in the boats, while the Supervising Committee, consisting of several eminent Naval men, stayed ashore, taking up residence in Victoria House on the Esplanade.

It had been planned to pay each man 4/- per launch, but the 160 launchers went on strike for more. Following negotiations they settled for 7/6d for every day they were employed, and the Trials got underway on Saturday 13 February. They continued when bad weather permitted until mid-April with a gap of some weeks when the weather was too settled. These spells of fine weather were not wasted however; they were used for testing various types of equipment.

The local press reported the happenings very fully, on one occasion from the deck of the paddle tug **Despatch** stationed near the Holm Sand. A *Lowestoft Journal* reporter wrote "that for three mortal hours, in the interests of the British public, they had braved the horrors of a turbulent sea; the numbing cold of an Arctic winter; a drenching rain, varied with blinding showers of salt spray, and the marrow-chilling blasts of a Lowestoft nor'easter, from the exposed bridge of a tug possessing the friskiness of a colt, in the trough of the ocean!"

Things dragged on and in mid-April everyone was fed up, and so, after a long spell of good weather the final day was 16 April. One reporter wrote, "The maritime vocabulary of the unfortunate local reporters now presents a singularly limp and exhausted appearance. Their billows no longer bound joyously, nor do the hillocks of violet tinted foam crested surf frisk like little lambs."

* * * * * * *

While the trials were in progress the Lowestoft station had only one service call. It was answered by the 36ft Norfolk and Suffolk boat *Husband* on relief duty. On 19 March the smack **The Bates Family** struck the Newcome Sand twice and the skipper burnt flares for a lifeboat. Coxswain Capps launched at 7.25pm and fired a green star shell to show that he had done so. The lifeboat was towed out by the **Rainbow** and as they cleared the piers an incoming smack was hailed to find out if they had seen anything. There was no reply from the vessel, which it later transpired was the "casualty". Consequently after an extensive search the lifeboat returned to harbour. The *Lowestoft Journal* of 26 March remarked that "the celerity with which the crew manned the lifeboat reminded one of the good old days."

On looking through the service lists in this book the reader will see time and again "No service(ns)". Two words which often concealed many hours of strenuous efforts on the part of the lifeboat crew, launchers and tug crew, all to no avail.

At about 1115pm on Tuesday 4 October 1892 rocket signals were fired from the **Corton** lightvessel indicating a vessel needing assistance. The *Samuel Plimsoll* launched into heavy seas and torrential rain and ran down in a northerly direction, but failed to find any trace of a vessel needing help. She put about and closed the lightvessel for more news. They were told that flares had been seen bearing WNW, but a further careful search revealed nothing. Fortunately near the **St. Nicholas** lightvessel the lifeboat fell in with the tug **Despatch** and got a tow back to Lowestoft arriving at about 3am. It later became apparent that the three-masted schooner **Jubilee** of Harwich collided with the Newcastle vessel **Teckla** in Corton Roads, the latter being badly damaged. She was helped by two Yarmouth tugs and the Gorleston lifeboat.

Such an event clearly shows the difficulties caused by the lack of any useful form of communication. Two lifeboats, three tugs and two other vessels only a mile or two apart, but nobody could know what was happening, with the result that much effort and risk was undertaken.

For the remainder of 1892 the *Samuel Plimsoll* only carried out four services, three were 'no service' and the fourth was 'assisted', though many onlookers claimed that the lifeboat just got in the way. The smack LT302 **Hiram**, owned by C Williams was carried against the North Extension by a strong ebb tide when outward bound. Two crew were washed overboard but rescued by the tug **Despatch**. A letter in the *Lowestoft Journal* of 10 December said "the tug was hampered by the lifeboat which was utterly useless in the circumstances." The following week another letter claimed that "the people on the extension got the smack off, not the tug and Mr Williams paid them like a gentleman for their services and also rewarded the lifeboat crew." The RNLI report says that the lifeboat got a line between tug and smack which was refloated.

Readers of Part 1 will recall, how in 1807 the Suffolk Humane Society set up a lifeboat at Lowestoft - the *Frances Ann* - and administered her until 1855 when the London Institution took over. In April 1892 the last meeting of the SHS was held in the Town Council Chambers on 12 April. Five of the 24 subscribers were present - J Peto Esq JP was Chairman and the others were Frederick Morse Esq (Treasurer), G Edwards Esq JP, Mr A Stebbings and Mr T E Thirtle. It was stated that cheques had been sent and receipts received from, The Royal Humane Society (£100), Lowestoft Hospital (£50), Lowestoft Widows and Orphans Permanent Funds (£100), and for the balance which went to the Lowestoft Fishermens' and Sailors' Home (£431 19s.10d). Mr G Edwards then moved that "the minute books, cash books and all other documents of the Society be placed in a tin box and handed over to the Trustees of the Fishermens' and Sailors' Home." This was agreed. Although the receipt of the cheque is recorded in the Minutes of the Home, there is no mention of the tin box of books, which is curious as F Morse Esq was Chairman and T E Thirtle one of the trustees at the time. When the Sailors' Home closed at the start of World War II, their records and some from the Sailors' Bethel were sent inland for safety. They would have been better left as the safe place was badly damaged and the papers so badly damaged by water that they were destroyed on a bonfire. Whether that included the records of the Suffolk Humane Society it has not been possible to find out.

In early January 1893 the saving of a vessel and her crew led to some acrimonious letters in the local press. On 15 January the barge **Mystery** of Harwich with timber for Newcastle grounded on Pakefield beach after losing her rudder in the Gat. She was towed off by the tug **Rainbow** and taken into Lowestoft harbour after members of the Pakefield lifeboat crew were put on board to assist. In the *Lowestoft Journal* of 21 January George Warford, Coxswain of the Pakefield boat, claimed that while he was on the barge she was boarded by Lowestoft lifeboatmen one of whom threatened to throw him overboard. Nothing like that had ever happened to him in his 31 years he said. Later in another letter he refused to name the person, but said that the young man should apologise. A letter from the North Roads Company said the man was not one of their group.

In August 1893 the London steamer **Erasmus Wilson** was again in trouble off Lowestoft. It will be recalled that in September 1886 she was in collision in the Stanford Channel with the **Lord Alfred Paget**, and was beached for repairs on the South beach. This time she went on the Newcome sand just opposite the harbour entrance. The Old Company of Beachmen were engaged to get her off with the help of the tugs **Rainbow** and **Imperial**. The *Lowestoft Journal* of 12 August reported that the new lifeboat went out under Coxswain Capps "..for some unknown reason.." That reason was mentioned in the Annual Report of the Branch published in early 1894. The lifeboat was a new one just received on station and the crew had launched to carry out a series of trials to familiarise themselves with the boat. They had a look at the steamer as a matter of routine.

This new boat *Stock Exchange* was built by Beeching Bros at Great Yarmouth to replace the earlier boat of the same name which had been rejected by the Lowestoft beachmen early in the lifeboat trials the previous year. She was 46ft long with a beam of 12ft 9 inches and rowed 14 oars like the earlier boat. The old *Stock Exchange* was taken to Beechings yard at Yarmouth and alterations were made to her. She was taken over by the Gorleston lifeboatmen and renamed *Mark Lane*, when she was said then to be "one of the finest boats in the Institution".

A real rescue took place on 18 November 1893, when the Lynn schooner **Marie** owned by R J Lydal foundered off the town. She was bound from London to Middlesborough and tried to make Lowestoft in bad weather. Unfortunately she struck the north extension and drifted south burning flares. The *Stock Exchange*, which was already manned, immediately put out and eventually managed to take off the Captain and crew of four. The unmanned vessel is thought later to have collided with another vessel, and she is reported in the wreck register to have foundered. Later the same day the lifeboat was towed out by the **Despatch** to the Hull ketch **Dayspring**. She was near the SW Newcome buoy and in danger of being driven onto the sand. The skipper and crew of two were safely taken off, and after landing the men, the tug and lifeboat went out again and towed the ketch into harbour. They were awarded £40 each as salvage.

Not content with saving eight lives on the 18th, the lifeboat was out again next day. The Grimsby cod smack GY640 **Sir Wilfred Lawson**, making for the harbour, hit the north extension and missed the harbour entrance. She drifted down the side of the South pier and stranded on the beach opposite the Royal Hotel where she was swept by breakers. Her Master, James Craske, and the crew of six were taken off. The smack was later towed off, but had received such a pounding from the seas that she was considered only fit to be broken up. The oak timber arising from the breaking up was sold by W T Balls on the Plain behind Pier Terrace in May and July 1894.

Then followed more "no service" launches until 14 October 1894 when the *Samuel Plimsoll* launched to the Liverpool steamer **Isabelle** (344 tons). She was bound to Trouville from the Tyne with coal, and when near the **Corton** lightvessel she signalled for help. The lightvessel also fired its gun and the lifeboat under Coxswain Capps was towed out by the **Rainbow** to find the ship helpless with the engine room flooded and the pumps choked. Captain Foley and his eleven men were rescued and the ship towed into Lowestoft. The lifeboat collected £117 11s as her share of the salvage.

A month later on the 14 November signals of distress were seen in Pakefield Gat. They were from the brigantine **Alf** of Mandal aground on the Newcome in a moderate SW gale. She was bound from Hernosund to Rio with planks and had been on her way for nearly a month. She had got as far as Dover but was driven back with her masts damaged and the rudder smashed. The *Samuel Plimsoll* was towed out by the tug **Despatch**, Pakefield launched their big No. 1 boat *Two Sisters Mary and Hannah* and the Kessingland No. 2 *Bolton* also ran down. Thanks to the tug the *Plimsoll* reached her first and took off the eight crew. The next morning the tug and lifeboat went out and managed to get her off the sands and into harbour for which the lifeboat was awarded £94 10s salvage. The **Alf** which had been built in Mandal in 1877 was too badly damaged to be worth repairing so she was broken up, and W T Balls, a local auctioneer sold some of her timbers the following April. A second portion was sold later at Smith's Marsh, opposite the Lake Lothing Inn in Denmark Road.

These rescues were followed by a slack spell with several "no service" launches, until the autumn of 1896. On 25 September the *Samuel Plimsoll* put out to the **Mystery** of Lowestoft which was dragging her anchors in the North Roads in a strong SSE gale. The lifeboat saved the crew of five and the vessel. Later the same day she put out to the 'boomie' barge **Sussex Belle** of London in trouble near Corton Sand. She put men on board the barge to help with the pumps while the **Despatch** towed her and the barge back to Lowestoft, saving the vessel and six including the Master's wife. In the book *'Sailing Barges'* by F G G Carr the author says she was built at Rye in 1892 and was considered a very fast boat.

During the weekend of 27/29 November 1897 the wind developed into a hard gale from the WNW. All the Lowestoft drifters were safely in but there were many vessels at anchor in the Roads, and soon several were flying flags for assistance. The tugs **Despatch, Rainbow, Imperial** and even the little **Resolute** were out assisting. About 9am on Monday the 29th the *Stock Exchange* was towed out by the **Despatch** to the schooner **Regina** of Jersey which had lost her anchors. She tried to make the entrance to the harbour but hit the South pier. Lifeboatmen who managed to get aboard, passed a rope to the tug and she was brought safely into harbour. Later at about 11am a small schooner drove down past the piers and smashed ashore mid-way along the Esplanade. Two of the crew were taken off by the lifeboat before she beached and the rest were helped ashore by some beachmen. The vessel was the 53 ton **Despatch** of Hull, owned by J Varley and she was soon a heap of wreckage. Later on the lifeboat was towed out to the Plymouth schooner **Broughty Castle** bound from her home port to Hull with china clay. She had already lost her sails so lifeboatmen were put aboard to help the tired crew get tow ropes fixed up and wreckage cleared. On the way in the schooner was in collision with another vessel at anchor, and lost her mainmast. However, she was saved with her crew of four.

Other lifeboats in the area were also busy and some came into Lowestoft. The steam lifeboat *City of Glasgow* stationed at Gorleston for six months trial put into the trawl dock after towing the ketch **Lord Nelson** from the **Cross Sand** lightvessel, while the old lifeboat *The Stock Exchange*, now *Mark Lane*, came in to land shipwrecked seamen, being unable to get into Gorleston. The Pakefield boat *Two Sisters Mary and Hannah* was also out and saved several crews. Because the wind hád by then gone NW, she had to run to Harwich with the survivors. This north-westerly wind resulted in the highest tide on record. Long before high water, the trawl and tug piers were covered, fish market flooded, some of the inner harbour quays under water, St. John's Church flooded and breakers were coming over the Esplanade into the Royal Hotel gardens. The wind was reported at Force 10.

Late in the winter of 1897/98 three vessels went ashore during the night of 31 March at Corton and Hopton. The Yarmouth smack **Betsy** smashed into the breakwater below Cliff House at Corton. Two of the crew were lost and the remaining four were taken off by the rocket apparatus. The ss **Abana** of Sunderland ran onto the beach at Hopton and was high and dry at low water with all her crew safe. The brigantine **Swallow** of Goole grounded only about 200 yards north of the Sunderland vessel and again her crew were rescued by the coastguards and their rocket apparatus.

The *Stock Exchange* was towed out by **Despatch** and the Gorleston lifeboat *Mark Lane* also put out. Neither was needed and so both lifeboats returned to Lowestoft after a very rough time.

William Jenner Capps, who had served as Coxswain since January 1883, made his final launch on 19 November 1900 when the smack LT474 **Leader** went onto the Newcome Sands while making for the harbour. The smack refloated before the lifeboat reached her.

During his period as Coxswain, William Capps had saved 131 lives. He died in February 1901 and is buried in Lowestoft cemetery.

Table 2

Services under Coxswain Capps 1883-1901

1883 *Samuel Plimsoll*

9 Jan	ketch, **John and Mary** of Goole, S Roads	assisted
	ketch, **Wonderful** of Goole, S Roads	assisted
2 Feb	schooner, **CTB of** Bristol,	ns
10 Feb	flares	ns
	Royal Albert	
6 Mar	schooner, **Jeannie** of Runcorn, Newcome	assisted
	Samuel Plimsoll	
19 Mar	schooner, **Fides** of Nyborg, S Roads	assisted
12 Dec	brig't, **Swift** of Rye, Cross Sand	assisted
17 Dec	trawler, **Magic** of Hull, near Corton	assisted

1884 *Samuel Plimsoll*

11 Oct	schooner, **Hannah** of Yarmouth, Corton	assisted
14 Nov	two Dutch luggers, Holm	ns
7 Dec	flares near Holm	ns
22 Dec	schooner, **Isabella** of N.Shields, Kessingland	ns

1885 *Samuel Plimsoll*

17 Jan	distress signals, Holm	ns
	trawler, **Snowdrop** of Ramsgate, Newcome	saved 5
19 Aug	a brig, Cross Sand	ns

1886 *Samuel Plimsoll*

3 Mar	schooner, **Caroline** of Faversham, Newcome	saved vessel + 7
10 Sep	ss **Erasmus Wilson** of London, Newcome	)landed 17 crew +
	ss **Lord Alfred Paget** of London, Newcome	)10 passengers

1887 *Samuel Plimsoll*

10 Feb	ss **Wilfred Lawson**, Corton Roads	ns
17 Mar	a smack, Newcome	ns
	Two Sisters Mary and Hannah	
30 Aug	schooner, **Maurice** of St.Vedast, Newcome	ns

1888 *Two Sisters Mary and Hannah*

21 Feb	brig, **Messenger** of Yarmouth, N Roads	stood by
13 Mar	smack, **Olive Branch** (LT258), drifting	assisted
17 Mar	Dutch galliot, Holm	ns
	Samuel Plimsoll	
19 Sep	unknown ss	ns
5 Nov	flares (bonfire on beach)	ns
7 Nov	launched but no details	ns
27 Nov	smack, **Undine** (LT289), N Extension	ns

1889 *Two Sisters Mary and Hannah*
2 Sep	smack, **Sir Alfred Gooch** (LT91), S Beach	stood by
7 Oct	schooner, **Lymington** of Harwich, Holm	saved 6
	brig't, **Marie**	ns
27 Oct	dandy - no details	ns
25 Nov	sloop, **Richard and Francis** of Goole, Newcome	stood by

1890 *Two Sisters Mary and Hannah*
26 Jan	schooner - no details	ns
11 Feb	signals from **Corton** LV, nothing found	ns
	The Stock Exchange	
19 Jul	fb **Don't Know** of Yarmouth, Corton	saved 1
	fb **Edith and Alice** of Yarmouth, Corton	saved 1
15 Aug	fb **Frolic** (LT296), Newcome	saved vessel
	small boat from **Frolic**, Newcome	saved 2
29 Oct	**Nile** - no details	
5 Dec	schooner, **Hannah** of Fowey, Holm	ns
6 Dec	ss **Empress** of Dundee, Barnard	ns

1891 *The Stock Exchange*
16 Jan	dandy, **Mary Farr** (LT384)	ns
29 Jan	smack, **Peace** (LT286), N Extension	saved 1
2 Apr	no details	
7 Apr	shrimper, **Early and Late**, Holm	not found
16 May	schooner, **Emma** of Padstow, Holm	stood by
	Samuel Plimsoll	
22 Oct	pilot cutter, **Alarm** showed flares	ns
26 Oct	drifting dredger	ns
30 Oct	no details	
11 Nov	lugger, **Paramount** of Hopeman, Holm	saved 2
2 Dec	schooner, **Belted Will** of Jersey, Newcome	assisted
13 Dec	smack, **Salem** of Ramsgate, off harbour entrance	ns

1892 *Husband*
19 Mar	smack, **The Bates Family** of Yarmouth, Newcome	ns
	Samuel Plimsoll	
27 Jul	smack, R350, Holm	ns
4 Oct	**Teckla** of Newcastle, Corton Roads	ns
19 Oct	a smack, Holm	ns
3 Dec	smack, **Hiram** (LT302), N Extension	assisted

1893 *Samuel Plimsoll*

10 Jan	signals from **Corton** LV	ns
15 Jan	barge, **Mystery** of Harwich, off Pakefield LH	saved 4

Stock Exchange

9 Aug	ss **Erasmus Wilson** of London, Newcome	ns
19 Sep	rockets seen - nothing found	
20 Oct	Smacks in dangerous position	ns
18 Nov	schooner, **Marie** of Kings Lynn, S Roads	saved 5
	ketch, **Dayspring** of Hull, Newcome	saved 3
	ketch, **Dayspring** of Hull, Newcome	saved vessel
19 Nov	smack, **Sir Wilfred Lawson** (GY640), S Beach	saved 7
1 Dec	smack, **Moggy** (LT37), Ness Point	ns
25 Dec	smack, **Esther** (LT195), S Beach	stood by

1894 *Stock Exchange*

3 Jan	Two smacks showing flares, outer channel	ns
8 Mar	smack, **Cleopatra** (LT277), Inner shoal	stood by

Samuel Plimsoll

18 May	schooner, **Ann** of Goole, S Roads	ns
? May	unknown steamer, Holm	ns
14 Oct	ss **Isabelle** of Liverpool, Newcome	saved vessel + 12
27 Oct	a schooner, Newcome	ns
14 Nov	brig't, **Alf** of Mandal, Newcome	saved 8
15 Nov	brig't, **Alf** of Mandal, Newcome	saved vessel
22 Dec	brig't, **Adela** of Southampton, Stanford	ns

1895 *Samuel Plimsoll*

23 Jan	schooner, **Topaz**, Newcome	stood by

Stock Exchange

10 Nov	schooner, **Florence Louise** of Hull, Holm	ns
21 Nov	unknown steamer, Newcome	ns

1896 *Stock Exchange*

8 Jan	brig't, **Kelpie** of S.Shields, Newcome	assembled
18 Mar	schooner, **Martha** of Dunkirk, Newcome	assisted

Samuel Plimsoll

25 Sep	**Mystery** of Lowestoft, N Roads	saved vessel + 5
	barge, **Sussex Belle** of London, Corton	saved vessel + 5
15 Oct	smack, **Jolly Tar** (LT419), Pakefield	ns

1897 *Samuel Plimsoll*

23 Jan	signals from **Corton** LV	ns
19 Mar	shrimper, **Faith**, Newcome	saved vessel + 2

Stock Exchange

1 Sep	smack, **Samuel J Dobson** (LT634), N Beach	saved vessel + 5
29 Nov	schooner, **Despatch** of Hull, S Beach	saved 2
	schooner, **Regina** of Jersey, S Pier	assisted
	schooner, **Broughty Castle** of Plymouth, N Roads	saved vessel + 4

1898 *Stock Exchange*

31 Mar	brig, **Celerity** of Lowestoft - no details	
	smack, **Betsy** of Yarmouth Corton beach	ns
	ss **Abana** of Sunderland, Corton Beach	ns
	brig't, **Swallow** of Goole, Corton Beach	ns
14 Oct	schooner, **Dovey Belle** of Portmadoc	ns

1899   No launches

1900 *Samuel Plimsoll*

15 May	ss **Skulda** of Grangemouth, Newcome	saved vessel + 17
	Stock Exchange	
19 Nov	smack, **Leader** (LT474), Newcome	ns

Coxswain William Capps, he was in charge of
Lowestoft lifeboats from 1883 until 1901.
(*PLRS Collection*)

The ss **Erasmus Wilson** of London beached on Lowestoft South beach on 10 September 1886 following a collision.
(*PLRS Collection*)

RNLB *Two Sisters Mary and Hannah* (ON23),
stationed at Lowestoft from 1886 until 1890 while
problems with the Pakefield boathouses were sorted out.
(*J W Mitchley Collection*)

RNLB *The Stock Exchange* (ON288), stationed at
Lowestoft from 1890 until 1892
(*J W Mitchley Collection*)

RNLB **Stock Exchange** (ON356), stationed at
Lowestoft from 1893 until 1918

(*J W Mitchley Collection*)

Chapter 3

Coxswain Mewse 1901-1911

Edwardian Times

John Mewse who had been 2nd Coxswain since January 1896 was appointed Coxswain on 13 March 1901, and Sam Turrell the second. Mewse made his first launch in charge on 30 March 1901 when the schooner **Elizabeth** of London was seen running through the Stanford Channel with a flag in the rigging. The *Stock Exchange* was towed out by the tug **Despatch** and caught up with the ship off Hopton. It turned out that she was signalling for a tug but the flag halliard got jammed and they could neither raise nor lower the signal. It is recorded that though the vessel was bound for Great Yarmouth, £10 was awarded to the lifeboat and the tug for the attempted service.

A tragic episode in 1902 again caused questions to be asked of the livesaving services at Lowestoft and pointed to shortcomings in the local organisation.

On 4 November the sailing drifter **Defender** was heading for Lowestoft with 12 lasts of herring on board when she struck the Barnard Sand. The crew lit flares, but the vessel knocked off and began to fill and so the skipper ran her ashore on the South beach close to the Empire Hotel at about 6.30pm. The flares had been seen at Kessingland but not Lowestoft; the Kessingland boat did not launch. The lifeboat slipway at Pakefield was obstructed by large blocks of concrete and so their boat could not get away either. Witnesses on the promenade saw the vessel come ashore and one of them, Dr H M Evans who lived nearby, went home and telephoned the Coastguard, he also collected a bottle of brandy and hurried back. Three crew were pulled ashore out of the breakers and taken to the Doctor's house. The coastguard rocket apparatus arrived, but the wind was adverse and they could not get lines aboard her. In any case by now she was broadside on and almost submerged. The lifeboat was not launched before almost 8.30pm and owing to poor lights being shown at the scene by the coastguard she was towed further to the south before turning north to anchor off the Empire Hotel. The Hotel must not have had much seaward-facing lighting since the Coxswain only saw the outline of the building against the night-sky after he turned northward. There were only the three survivors out of seven.

The *Lowestoft Journal* of 8 November said there was a strong body of opinion that the lifeboat ought to have been called earlier, and that a public enquiry was needed to answer various questions.

The body of one of the crew was recovered the day following the wreck and an inquest was opened a few days later. The Mate, Alfred Coleman, said they were running up Pakefield Gat when they hit the sands and started to fill. Having burnt two flares (clothes soaked in turpentine) the skipper suggested running for the beach which they did. In answer to the Coroner (Mr C W Chaston) the Mate said there was only one lifebelt on board. There was much questioning of witnesses which showed that the coastguards had arrived at about 7.10pm and set up the rocket apparatus. A local boatowner, John Jenner, said he told the coastguards that the lifeboat was needed. He said they only had a poor light at the scene. He felt if the lifeboat had been called sooner all could have been saved. Robert Strowger, Coxswain of the Kessingland boat, gave evidence that he saw the flares and ran his boat down the beach. Discussions with the Secretary of the local RNLI Branch stopped the launch, with the Secretary, Mr Hicks, who was also the local Chief Officer of Coastguard for Kessingland, going to telephone the Lowestoft coastguard.

The 2nd Coxswain of Pakefield said they could not launch because broken pieces of seawall obstructed the slipway. The RNLI HQ knew of the position, but there had been discussion with the Rural District Council who felt the slipway to be a public right of way and therefore the RNLI felt it the duty of the RDC to clear the slip.

Henry George Reynolds, Landlord of the East of England Tavern in Whapload Road, said he was a member of the Beach Company and sometimes manned the lifeboat. At about 7.45pm, near the bridge, he saw George Colby who had said to him "For God's sake Harry, rouse the lads out and get the lifeboat. There is a wreck and poor fellows will be drowned." Reynolds ran to Coxswain Mewse's house in Whapload Road seeing him at 7.55pm and from there he went to the signaller to get the signal put up. He then helped with the launch and the boat got away about 8.25pm. He added to his evidence that he had never known the coastguard call out the lifeboat, "they always keep to themselves." Coxswain Mewse gave evidence and seemed of the opinion of many, that if he had been called earlier the crew could have been saved. He said "The coastguard do not call us. They called us the following night, but it is the first time for a very long while."

Police Inspector Ruffles gave evidence as to messages he received and that he called the coastguard at 6.57pm but the operator could get no reply. When he arrived at the scene the coastguard had only small handheld flares which burnt till they burnt the hand of the man holding it, when another was lit. The Chief Officer of the Coastguard, Charles Johnson said he had lights burning as the lifeboat passed and that he did regard it as part of coastguard duties to call the lifeboat. He admitted that he had not done so on this occasion nor had he ordered it done.

The jury returned verdicts of "death by drowning". They felt the Coastguard Chief Officer was to blame in his eagerness to get to the wreck for omitting to call the lifeboat. They recommended that powerful lights be used ashore at the scene and that an alarm signal be set up for calling the lifeboat. They felt a surf boat should be stationed between Kessingland and Lowestoft and that the blockage at Pakefield slip should be removed. The jury gave their fees for the widows and orphans of the disaster.

On the night of 28/29 March 1904 the Newcome Sands were the scene of a difficult rescue. At about midnight the smack LT394 **Industry** went aground in heavy weather. With great difficulty the *Stock Exchange* managed to get off the crew of five. They were landed in the harbour and the tug **Lowestoft** towed her out again. Lifeboatmen went on board, made fast a tow rope and the smack was towed off and taken into harbour. In going alongside the lifeboat was damaged and had to be taken off service. She went to Chambers yard for repairs where other damage was found. The total cost was £112. Salvage was paid by the Smack Insurance Society of £150 shared by tug and lifeboat. The **Industry** was sold in 1907 to Sweden and returned to this country in 1987 to take parties for cruises round the Western Isles where she is now under the name of **Lorne Leader** based near Oban.

In January 1905 the brig **Celerity**, owned by J S Sterry of Lowestoft, was lying off Corton on the evening of Sunday the 15th when she signalled for help. The crew mustered but word reached them that the Gorleston steam lifeboat *James Stevens No. 3* had launched and so the *Samuel Plimsoll* did not go. After much discussion **Celerity's** crew left her and were taken to Gorleston. On the Monday Mr Sterry went to Gorleston and made arrangements for his crew to be taken back. The next day a Yarmouth tug went out with some beachmen who apparently refused to go aboard the ship. Mr Sterry and his crew arrived just as the tug **United Services** was starting the tow. Mr. Sterry ordered his crew aboard and they took charge but only after threats of dire consequences if the tug did not desist. The tug crew had already by this time lost two anchors from the **Celerity**. The tug Company claimed for salvage, but Sterry sued them for piracy and won damages of £35.

A few months later the Newcome Sands saw another salvage job which turned out well for the lifeboat. On 19 April the ss **Spring** of Christiania (Oslo), loaded with sleepers for the Great Eastern Railway Coy., ran onto the Newcome almost opposite the Low light. The harbour tugs **Despatch** and **Imperial** went out, the latter towing the *Samuel Plimsoll*. Some of the crew went onto the steamer and while some helped jettison the deck cargo the rest rigged up the tow line. Later, on a rising tide, the steamer came off and was brought into Lowestoft. The Railway Company records show that the tug was paid £311 10s, with the same amount for the lifeboat. A good days' work for the lifeboat.

As things turned out this was the last launch for the much loved *Samuel Plimsoll*. In July 1905 Coxswain Mewse and a small crew took her down to the Thames Ironworks at Blackwall, London where the Institution was to use her for motor trials. In her time at Lowestoft she was credited with 83 service launches, 30 vessels saved and 165 persons rescued. Having handed her over, Mewse and his men took over the new lifeboat *Kentwell* which had just been completed at the yard. She was the first ever lifeboat for Lowestoft not to have been built in either the town or in Yarmouth. However she was still a Norfolk and Suffolk type 46 ft long, a beam of 12 ft with two drop keels, four water ballast tanks and 14 oars. She cost £2197 which was met by the generous bequest of the late Mrs Eliza Amelia Moore of Onslow Square, London. The name was her choice.

The first launch for the new boat was on 11 November 1905. In the local Branch records it is shown as an "attempted service to an unknown small boat." A week later she was again unable to help. On 18 November the lugger BF603 **Maggie May** was wrecked on the spur groyne running off from the South pier. The gunboat **HMS Halcyon** was moored off the pier in such a place as to cause the lugger to come in on a course which prevented her from rounding the South pier head successfully. She fell off and drifted down the side. The Life Saving Apparatus was soon in action but the coastguards were unable to get a line across the pitching boat. Eventually, an angler, Mr. Groom, made a fine cast and his line went right over the boat. Soon the light line was across followed by the breeches buoy. The men were brought safely to the pier. By next morning the **Maggie May** had gone to pieces, just floating wreckage remaining. The Institution sent down £35 7s.6d for this service, but £3 was sent back marked "amount disallowed, two men drunk on duty." Jack Mitchley annotated his record 'the only time I have ever come across such a note.' Not an auspicious start for the new boat.

On 23 November the *Kentwell* was out again, this time to the smack LT12 **New Boy**. Coming in on a very calm day, the tide carried her past the harbour entrance and she grounded on the spur groyne not far from the wreck of the **Maggie May**. An anchor was run out from the smack to hold her off the beach and the crew of five were taken off. The *Lowestoft Journal* of 25 November reported that she gradually dragged towards the South pier and eventually was pounding against it. On the day after, she was towed off by the **Lowestoft**, full of water, pumped out and taken into harbour. The lifeboat sustained two holes in the cork belting and was taken for repair to Chambers yard.

On 20 May 1906 the sailing cutter **Themis** of London lost her sails and suffered damage at the back of Corton Sands. The *Kentwell* was towed out by **Despatch** and put two men aboard. After much difficulty the cutter successfully floated off and the tug towed her and the lifeboat back to harbour. The **Themis** was a one time tender to the training ship **Shaftesbury** and was on her way to Hull for conversion to a yacht. The salvage case was settled for £70 - no note of how much for the lifeboat.

In 1907 there was a launch which caused plenty of discussion in Committee. On 13 April the Faversham schooner **Caledonia** from Seaham for Whitstable with coal was wrecked on the Newcome in a strong ENE gale which made it impossible for the *Stock Exchange* to get out without assistance. She was towed out by the **Despatch** (Capt. Sam Sterry). Because of the sandbanks and the deep draught of the tug they went down the Roads and through the Stanford Channel, round the sands and to the windward of the wreck. As they were nearing the casualty two of her crew were swept off and lost. The lifeboat saved the remaining three, but was damaged when the ship's mainmast fell on her. It is reported that the Captain (very exhausted) and the two crew members were taken to the Sailors' Home and that the Captain's wife came up from Faversham, the two journeying home together. The Honorary Secretary in his report for 1907 says "This instance, I think, points to the great value of the motor lifeboats which have been placed on several stations by the Institution, as in cases where the wind and tide are against a sailing boat the motor boat can make straight to the wreck across the sands instead of having to take the course of the tug, thus effecting a great saving of time, which is of course, of the greatest importance. As tugs have to be employed on nearly every occasion the boats are launched it is to my mind a question worth considering by the Committee as to whether they approach the Institution with a view to a motor boat being allotted to this station." There is no record of the Committee making such an approach. It was another 14 years before a motor boat came here.

It was a case of third time unlucky on 9 January 1908 when the brig **Celerity** of Lowestoft went on the North beach abreast of the High Street Rectory. In March 1898 and again in January 1905 either the Lowestoft or Gorleston lifeboat was launched to her assistance. This time she broke from her anchors in the North Roads in a strong northerly gale. The *Kentwell* was towed out through mountainous seas by the **Despatch** the *Lowestoft Journal* adding "of which that brave old sea dog, the hero of many a hazardous trip, Capt. Sam Sterry was in charge." The Life Saving Apparatus attended and managed after some difficulty to get a line across the wreck and get the crew ashore. That was fortunate since the lifeboat was not able to get near enough to be of any practicable help.

On Friday 3 September 1909 the ss **Longwood** of Glasgow left the Thames in water ballast for the Tyne to be repaired. About five hours later she grounded on Maplin Sand, but came off later. At about 5am the following morning she started to make water, the pumps could not cope and the boiler fires were drawn. She also took a list to starboard until the rails were at water level. Some of the crew put off in a boat and were taken on board the smack **Viator** which stood by. One of Watkins tugs the **Wild Rose** of Gravesend and the Lowestoft tugs **Lowestoft** and **Despatch** went to her and the services of the **Lowestoft** were accepted. A pilot was taken out and the vessel brought into Lowestoft and put alongside the tug pier, pumped out and taken through the bridge the next day, Sunday. Thus reported the *Lowestoft Journal* adding later that nothing was found to be wrong with her.

A Board of Trade Enquiry was held in Newcastle on the 25th. It reported:

> "On August 27 left Dunkirk and ran into sea wall. Damage repaired and a certificate of seaworthiness issued. Left for London with general cargo on 30 August and left the Thames on 3 September for Newcastle. Just after Gravesend a pin fell out of steering gear and was replaced, and later near the **Mouse** lightvessel it had to be replaced again. Soon after she ran onto the Mouse Bank. Refloated later and found to be making water and starting to list. Some crew left and tugs from Lowestoft arrived, but help declined. Later a tow

was taken up from the **Lowestoft** and she arrived at Lowestoft where she was pumped out and found to be tight. Under new Chief and 2nd Engineers the vessel sailed to the Tyne under her own power, was docked and no damage was found to her skin. In the last 10 years over £11000 had been spent on the vessel."

The Judgement was:

"The Master in default for not making efforts to find cause of the inflow of water nor to stem it and for not heading the vessel to shore while power remained and for refusing assistance when the ship was sinking and in urgent need of help. The Chief Engineer in default for not keeping suction pipes clear and the pumping arrangements and water tight doors in good order, for not taking steps to prevent inflow of water and for not making every possible effort to keep it down. Master to pay £50 and Chief Engineer £40 towards costs of enquiry."

I wonder if this might be a case of ballast water getting where it should not?

John Mewse made his last service launch on 12 January 1911 having reached the RNLI age for retirement of Coxswains. This was to the Rochester sailing barge **Pioneer** which was wrecked on Colman's breakwater at Corton. The crew of three were saved by the coastguards and their rocket apparatus. The *Kentwell* had been towed out by the tug **Lowestoft** under Capt. Vrolyk, but was not needed.

During his service as Coxswain John Mewse made 51 launches and saved 34 lives.

Table 3

Services under Coxswain Mewse 1901-1911

1901 *Stock Exchange*
30 Mar	schooner, **Elizabeth** of London	ns
15 May	ss **Martha** of Danzig, N Beach	ns
	Samuel Plimsoll	
14 Nov	ketch, **Clarence** of Bridgwater	ns

1902 *Samuel Plimsoll*
4 Nov	drifter, **Defender** (LT701), S Beach	ns
5 Nov	unknown vessel	ns
26 Nov	sloop, **Pilot**, N Roads	ns

1903 *Stock Exchange*
4 Aug	Pilot boat	ns
28 Nov	flares	ns
7 Dec	smack, **Saluts**, Ness Point	ns

1904 *Stock Exchange*
25 Mar	trawler, **Frobisher** (YH1029), Barnard	ns
28 Mar	smack, **Industry** (LT394), Newcome	saved 5
29 Mar	smack, **Industry** (LT394), Newcome	saved vessel
	Samuel Plimsoll	
1 Sep	trawler, **Paula Bertha** of Ostend, Holm	saved vessel + 6
30 Oct	ss **Tees** - no details	ns
9 Nov	barge, **Tintara** of London	stood by
30 Dec	schooner, **Nancy** of Goole, Holm	assisted
	lugger, **Mercurius** of Holland	ns

1905 *Samuel Plimsoll*
15 Jan	brig, **Celerity** of Lowestoft, Corton Roads	ns
14 Mar	unknown vessel	ns
21 Mar	unknown vessel	ns
19 Apr	ss **Spring** of Christiania, Newcome	assisted
	Stock Exchange	
9 Sep	smack, **Maude** (LT126), off Pakefield	assisted
24 Sep	smack, **Lily Maud** (LT501), S Beach	assisted
	Kentwell	
11 Nov	small boat	ns
18 Nov	fb **Maggie May** (BF603), S Beach	ns
23 Nov	smack, **New Boy** (LT12), S Beach	saved 5

1906 *Kentwell*

Date	Vessel	Outcome
12 Jan	**Challenger**	assembly
	smack, **Sweet Hope** (LT157), N Beach	assembly
20 May	cutter, **Themis** of London, Corton sand	saved vessel + 4
	Stock Exchange	
29 Jun	shrimper, **Reliance**	ns
3 Jul	**Sea Bird** - no details	ns
5 Nov	st **Lord Roberts** of Hull, Holm	stood by
15 Nov	unknown vessel	ns

1907 *Stock Exchange*

Date	Vessel	Outcome
23 Jan	smack, **Nancy** (LT41), S Pier	stood by
13 Apr	schooner, **Caledonia** of Faversham, Newcome	saved 3

1908 *Kentwell*

Date	Vessel	Outcome
9 Jan	brig, **Celerity** of Lowestoft, N Beach	ns
10 Jan	schooner, **Janet** of Carnarvon, Holm	assisted
22 Feb	smack, **Arizona** (LT297), S Roads	stood by
	Stock Exchange	
20 Jul	smack, **Integrity** (LT930), Holm	saved vessel + 6
15 Aug	**Ruby** - no details	
21 Oct	ss **Bow**, Newcome	stood by
22 Oct	ss **Meitzing** of Danzig, Newcome	stood by
7 Nov	drifter, **Faithful** (INS262), N Beach	stood by

1909 *Stock Exchange*

Date	Vessel	Outcome
8 Jan	ss **Pittan** of Russia	ns
	Kentwell	
16 Mar	ss **Marjorie** of Goole	ns
27 May	smack, **Majestic** (LT43), S Beach	saved 5
2 Jun	smack, **Marjorie** (LT239), no details	
	Stock Exchange	
2 Aug	longshore boats	stood by
4 Sep	ss **Longwood** of Glasgow	stood by
13 Oct	lugger, **Celtic** of Kirkcaldy, Newcome	ns
29 Oct	**Neptune** of Mariehamn, no details	
23 Dec	ss **Mercury** of Dundee, Newcome	stood by

1910 *Kentwell*

Date	Vessel	Outcome
1 Apr	unknown schooner - no details	
22 Aug	smack, **Young Harry** (LT288), Holm	stood by

1911 *Kentwell*

Date	Vessel	Outcome
12 Jan	barge, **Pioneer** of Rochester, Corton	ns

Coxswain John Mewse, he was in charge of Lowestoft
lifeboats from 1901 until 1911.
(*PLRS Collection*)

The sailing drifter **Defender** (LT701) ashore on Lowestoft South beach after striking the Barnard sands on 4 November 1902.
(*PLRS Collection*)

RNLB **Kentwell** (ON543), stationed at Lowestoft from 1905 until 1921.
(*PLRS Collection*)

The brig **Celerity** of Lowestoft ashore on Lowestoft
North beach 9 January 1908.
(*PLRS Collection*)

The ss **Longwood** of Glasgow in Lowestoft harbour in a sinking condition on 4 September 1909.
(*PLRS Collection*)

CHAPTER 4

Coxswain Swan 1911 - 1924

Part I - The Great War

When it came to choosing the next Coxswain John Thompson Sterry Swan the nominee of the Young Company of Beachmen received 100 votes against the 60 for George Ayers of the Old Company. John Swan had been Secretary of the New Young Company since its formation in 1892 and Coxswain of their crack yawl **Georgiana** from the same date. He also had a son and three brothers connected with the lifeboat. He was officially appointed on 18 January 1911 with George Ayers as his second Coxswain.

Two months later, on 19 March, he made his first launch as Coxswain to the smack LT173 **Express** near the Claremont Pier. The **Despatch** towed the **Kentwell** out and managed to get a line to the smack which she towed in. The tug returned to the lifeboat and towed her in as well. There followed a series of launches with not much action just "standing by" or "assisting".

Then there came a night in a storm. At 10am on 11 January 1913 they launched to the boomie barge **Alice Watts** of Harwich which was dragging her anchors and heading for Corton beach in a strong ESE wind. The **Kentwell** was towed out by the tug **Despatch** under Capt. Sterry and managed to reach the barge before she went ashore. John Swan dropped the anchor and veered down to the barge and despite being continually swamped by breaking seas, managed to put men aboard and take a hawser to the tug. The **Alice Watts** was pulled away from the shore and into harbour. The barge had been built in Ipswich in 1875 for John Watts and was named after his daughter.

The ESE wind rose to gale force and continued throughout the day. At about 4pm a vessel in the North Roads was seen burning flares for assistance. The **Despatch** towed **Kentwell** clear of the harbour but was then obliged to return to harbour, having received some damage in the **Alice Watts** rescue. The **Kentwell** proceeded under sail to the vessel which was the barge **Gladys** of Dover. The crew of three were taken off, but the tide and wind were against her so they could not get home. The harbour at Yarmouth was blocked by a sunken steamer **Gangeren** of Norway which had hit the North pier earlier in the month. There was nothing for it but to anchor and await an improvement. John Swan noted in his log book "the boat got under the sand and rode it out - it did blow". They got under way at daybreak and soon saw **Despatch** under George Munnings coming out to look for them. They had been at sea over 17 hours, exposed all the time to a whole gale with squalls of snow and rain and with virtually no protection. The men were numbed with cold and absolutely exhausted and must have been very relieved to be towed home. The Pakefield lifeboat *James Leath* had been out during the night searching for them because of fears for their safety. A fresh crew manned the *Kentwell*, took her out again and brought in the **Gladys** which had a cargo of tiles and was bound to London from the Humber. The Institution sent down £54 4s for the service, followed by an extra allowance of £7 2s.6d because of the arduous nature of the task. There was later an award of £34 10s for salvage. This job was the last for the well known Capt. Sam Sterry on the railway tugs before he retired.

The next half dozen or so launches were to fishing boats either on the beach or the Newcome, and were mostly salvage jobs. At one, probably that on 4 April 1913 to the smack LT1033 **Evolution** which ran ashore alongside a groyne on the North beach, the bow pudding and shield on the *Kentwell* was knocked off. John Swan, representing the lifeboatmen had to pay £4 6s for its replacement. Since the salvage for that job amounted to £95 he probably did not worry too much. Soon after, on 10 June, John Swan must have had a surprise since his own longshore boat LT625 **Surprise** was reported overdue. She had been out mackerel fishing when the wind got up to a strong SW which whipped up a nasty sea. The lifeboat found her some 12 miles out hanging on to her nets where she had been blown by the gale. Lifeboatmen went on board and helped haul the nets and by the time that was done the tug **Despatch** had turned up and towed both the *Stock Exchange* and the **Surprise** back to Lowestoft.

On 4 August 1914 war against Germany was declared. The *Lowestoft Journal* reported on 8 August the first effects. Skipper Pleasants of the smack LT696 **Loch Nevis** said the he had seen the German minelayer **Koningen Louise** being chased by a British light cruiser **HMS Amphion** and the 3rd Destroyer flotilla. There was also a full report of the Kessingland regatta, and a note that the German schooner **Fiducia** had been arrested in Yarmouth.

On 2 September the drifter LT1121 **Eyrie** was lost with all hands having struck a mine, and the following day LT322 **Linsdell** was mined. Some of her crew were picked up by the fleet minesweeper **HMS Speedy** which was herself mined later in the day. Another fleet minesweeper **HMS Halcyon** brought in some survivors whilst more came in aboard LT63 **Sussex County**. Near the end of the month three cruisers **HMS Hogue, HMS Aboukir** and **HMS Cressy** were torpedoed. They were the first ever British warships to be sunk by submarine action. Two Lowestoft smacks LT369 **JGC** under Skipper George Jacobs and LT153 **Coriander** under Skipper Tom Phillips, which were fishing in prohibited waters, picked up over 600 survivors between them, transferring the rescued to destroyers as necessary. The **JGC** brought her final batch of 34 to Lowestoft. About 5 miles outside the **Smith's Knoll** lightvessel she was met by the patrol vessel **HMS Spider** which towed her abreast of the harbour where the tug **Lowestoft** took over.

In October 1914 the Germans had invaded Belgium and the *Lowestoft Journal* reported on 17 October that Belgian refugees were beginning to arrive at the port on Ostend fishing smacks. About 25 boats had arrived on 15 October and some ran aground on the NE Newcome. The *Kentwell* went out under John Swan and took 35 men, women and children off two of them the O52 and O136 which were aground. As the tide made later they both came off. Jenkins took photographs of some of the Belgian boats in the inner harbour alongside **HMS Halcyon**. The pilot's motor boat also rescued some and the Institution sent down £2 5s for them.

The Lowestoft lifeboat had a slow start to her 'War Service', but trouble soon came in the shape of **HMS Spider** mentioned above. On 21 November she brought up in the South Roads. During the night the wind increased from the NE and so it was decided to move to the North Roads for better shelter from the banks. Unfortunately, in the dark, she ran aground on the North beach opposite the Old Company's Shed and within sight of the Coastguard station. The rocket apparatus went and managed to get their fifth shot onto the ship. The *Kentwell* had by now arrived. Swan let go his anchor and tried to veer down on the wreck, but twice he failed, and so, having buoyed the anchor, he set the foresail and sailed her in. They struck the flat heavily, lowered the sail which brought the lifeboat head to sea and fell alongside the wheelhouse where all the crew had gathered. They were soon in the boat, which then sailed over the flat again, recovered the anchor and landed the survivors in the harbour. The **Spider** was wrecked and was to cause trouble for many years. The whole rescue as described by Coxswain Swan sounds so very simple, but it all took place in the early hours of the morning, in pitch dark with gale force winds in an open boat with heavy seas constantly breaking over wreck and rescuer.

The gear was still being stowed from this service when the Coxswain saw another steamer strike the Newcome and the crew take to the rigging. He assembled his crew again and put out once more to the latest casualty. The sea had increased to what John Swan described as "..a tremendous heavy sea.." Arriving at the vessel which proved to be another of His Majesty's Ships the **Condor**, they anchored and veered down to the wreck. This proved to be a dangerous and slow job since the crew were in the rigging and every time a man was taken off, the lifeboat had to be hauled away. It was repeated until all the crew of nine had been taken off. Heavy seas were breaking over the lifeboat, and owing to the position of the **Condor** on the sands the lifeboat struck her no less than five times. Fortunately there was no serious damage. This service took place in broad daylight and directly opposite the town. In the Coxswain's report he says "Thousands of people watched us from the shore. We got a right royal reception when we arrived back". Jack Mitchley noted that "one well known book on Ships of the Royal Navy reports this wreck as being in the Firth of Forth".

Captain Alfred Ellison RN who was Commodore of the Lowestoft Naval Base and had his HQ in the Pier Pavillion, asked Swan to call on him. He congratulated the Coxswain personally on his tremendous work that day. Captain Ellison had previously been Commanding Officer of **HMS Halcyon** the fleet minesweeper which had been based at Lowestoft at the start of the war.

The **Spider** had been built by Cochranes of Selby in 1908 as the **Assyrian**. She was bought by the Admiralty in April 1909 for conversion to a minesweeper and fitted with a 6 pounder. On 31 March 1915 her wreck was sold on Admiralty orders by Hobson & Co and was bought by Mr A Gouldby for £70. He was never able to clear it and her remains caused trouble for many years.

In 1905 Mr T Bascomb had GY85 **Condor** built at Beverley in Yorkshire. She was taken up by the Admiralty in 1914 and fitted with the usual 6 pounder. In 1918 the Admiralty sold the wreck to a Mr Christie for £200. He paid out £2000 on salvage work, but while waiting for heavy lifting gear Trinity House blew the remains up as a danger to shipping. They were sued by Christie but it has not proved possible to find the result of the case.

'Jack' Swan was awarded the Institution's Silver medal and framed Vellum for the service to **Condor**. The Committee of Management were of the opinion that it had been "an exceptionally arduous service calling for fine seamanship and great courage". These were presented to him at the Annual Meeting of the RNLI in London during March 1915. There was also an extra 15/- per man.

Despite wartime conditions small sailing craft were still about, using the inshore channel and finding the sandbanks getting in the way. On 2 February 1915 the sailing barge **Sirdar** of Grays went on the Newcome. She was on her way from Harwich to Yarmouth with rice and was completely wrecked. The *Kentwell* was towed out by the **Lowestoft** and rescued the crew of two.

The next call is something of a mystery. The 1915 Annual Report of the Lowestoft Branch reports the *Kentwell* launched to the tanker **San Ricardo** on 15 March. There is no mention of it in John Swan's logbook, nor in the local press. In the RNLI *Journal* the Gorleston No.1 boat *Mark Lane* is recorded as attending the tanker, aground on the north Holm Sand, along with the *Kentwell*. Strangely the RNLI records show that no payment was requested by Lowestoft - no reason is given. The Great Eastern Railway Coy., records show that a fully laden tanker of 6460 tons ran onto Corton Sand. No date is given, but a salvage award in February 1917 shows that all the local GER tugs were out on the job. The **Lowestoft** was awarded £862 0s.5d; **Despatch** £642 1s.10d: **May** £375 3s; **Imperial** £214 14s; and **Resolute** £161 10s; a total of £2255 9s.3d. There is no mention of the lifeboat, but it seems very unlikely that she was not involved with all those tugs, in standing by, passing hawsers and being generally useful.

The GER tugs were also used in the next lifeboat service. The Greenock steamer **Glenpark** was bound from Hartlepool to Cowes with coal when she stranded on the Holm Sand on 18 April 1915. Three GER tugs including the **Lowestoft**, the lifeboat *Stock Exchange* and the Beachmen salvaged the vessel. When she first went ashore she was "got" by the Old Company's gig, and Coxswain Swan was Young Company, which caused some controversy. When any money for launching or salvage was received it was "doled" out and any sick members were always included. In this case the salvage money was passed to the first Company on the scene - the Old Company. They doled it out but did not include sick members of the Young Company. John Swan in his log reported that they had to get a lawyer to sort it out. "It was a ruffled shame", he said.

It may seem strange to us that there often seemed to be problems over salvage money, or indeed that salvage seemed to figure large in the work of lifeboat, tugs and beachmen. We need to remember, I think, that times for the ordinary man were hard and the men we are speaking of were ordinary in terms of wealth. Any chance to gain a few extra shillings had to be taken as a means of maintaining a reasonable standard for one's family; and they would be big families like as not. For the lifeboatmen saving lives always came first but if the opportunity arose to salvage a ship then why not, if the owners would pay to have their ship saved.

Sometimes owners were not so generous. On 27 May 1915 the *Stock Exchange* launched to the minesweeper **HMS Canton** which had run onto the Newcome Sand. She made two journeys, the second to act as the link between the ship and a tug. At the end of the year the Admiralty sent £25 to be shared between 20 men. As it was below the normal launching rate the Institution sent additional money. There was particular annoyance because the ship was new and valued at £13000. Governments do not change, it seems!

In its issue of 20 May 1915 the *Motor Boat* suggested that it was time the Lowestoft station had a motor lifeboat instead of the sailing one. Nothing happened though, and the two boats soldiered on.

On 13 August the Swedish steamer **Sverige** of Gefle was mined in the Stanford Channel. The Captain and most of the crew were brought ashore with three left on board. The **Stock Exchange** stood by all night and eventually, when the vessel settled down she took off the last three. The ship had been bound to London with deals, battens and boards to a value of £300. On 7 October what cargo had been salvaged was auctioned by Messrs Hobsons & Co on the wharf adjoining the Ice Works in Waveney Drive. The ship had been built in Sunderland in 1882 as the **Biscaye**, later she became the **Aval** and finally the **Sverige**. Her brass bell is in the Maritime Museum at Lowestoft.

The next casualty to be dealt with was on 27 October when the collier **Gar de Peē** of Cardiff grounded on the Holm Sand. She was *en route* to Nantes from Middlesborough with railway material. Two Yarmouth tugs and the **Despatch** and **Imperial** failed to shift her and they left about mid-day on the 28th. Before that, *Kentwell,* in worsening weather, had taken off the crew leaving the Master and Mate. She then helped lay a kedge anchor to prevent the ship driving further up the sands and took ashore a piece of the main steam pipe for repairs. During the night the weather worsened and the two on board burnt flares for assistance. The **Despatch** towed *Kentwell* out again and they found the ship had come off and was bouncing around quite a bit. Some lifeboatmen were put aboard and she was towed to the North Roads where the crew were put back aboard together with the repaired pipe. When this had been fitted she made for Grimsby under her own steam. Unfortunately a year later she was torpedoed and sunk 70 miles from the North Cape of Norway.

A month later on 29 November the 2510 ton **Framfield** of London went onto the Newcome and burnt flares for help as well as sending up rockets. It was blowing very hard from the SSW and the *Kentwell* was towed out and then made her way across the sands. They found the casualty lying very close to the masts of the **Sverige**. The lifeboat anchored and veered down and succeeded in taking off the 24 crew on a very black and stormy night. A shore party trained a searchlight on the wreck and that was a great help reported the Coxswain. After two hours or so the rescued men were landed ashore. On the following day the lifeboat took the Captain and crew back to try to get her off. The **Despatch** tried but could not move her, so lumpers were put aboard to jettison some of the cargo which was iron ore from North America. Later the Yarmouth tug **George Jewson** laid out a bower anchor and with the help of the tug **Fastnet** got her off about teatime on 1 December. The lifeboat was awarded £310 13s.5d with the tugs getting just over £1000.

On Boxing Day 1915 the steamer **Wharfdale** went on the Newcome and the *Kentwell* went out but the crew would not leave. Just as well since after about two hours she came off and the lifeboat returned to harbour in tow of the tug.

That completed the first full year of War Service with 15 launches and 51 saved.

On 23 February 1916 the Whitstable schooner **Carmenta** went ashore at Thorpeness a mile or so north of Aldeburgh. The Southwold lifeboat could not get to her and so the Naval Authorities sent for the lifeboats from Lowestoft and Kessingland. It was never made clear what the Navy thought the bigger boats could do that the smaller Southwold one could not. The *Kentwell* got as close as she could but the weather was so bad that after an hour and a half she had to pull away, and with the Kessingland boat was taken in tow of the **Lowestoft** which had laid further out. The gale was from the ENE with heavy snow squalls and the journey home must have been uncomfortable in the extreme for the tug and the two lifeboats.

Coxswain Swan records that it was said to be the worst gale since 1881. He was laid up for six weeks after a rope parted during the tow and caught one of his legs. The **Carmenta** eventually drove further up the beach and the crew were rescued by the rocket apparatus.

On 28 March 1916 two sailing ships, two steamers and a minesweeper **HMS Blacklyn** went on Corton beach. The Naval authorities ordered the launch of the *Kentwell* but the weather was so bad a crew could not be found, but even if men could have been found it is unlikely that they could have got out of the harbour. The following morning the wind had moderated and the *Kentwell* was towed down to one of the schooners. When they arrived they found that the coastguards with their rocket apparatus had rescued all the crews with the exception of that from the ship nearest Hopton. The Gorleston lifeboat *Mark Lane* had got them. When they returned, George Ayers the 2nd Coxswain who was in charge, was asked to go out to the minesweeper. They went out and helped the tug **Lowestoft** get her off the beach. Later in the year an award of £40 for salvage was received.

The East Anglian coastal waters were a favourite place for minelaying U-boats to work. On 10 July the 2338 ton steamer **Kara** which was *en route* to the Tyne in ballast, was mined off the Holm Sand. A minesweeper was despatched to take off the crew which she did, but then she ran aground on the Holm. The *Stock Exchange* launched under the 2nd Coxswain and took the 21 rescued men off the minesweeper leaving the tugs to pull her clear. The explosion had been heard in Gorleston and the volunteer lifeboat *Elizabeth Simpson* was towed out by the tug **George Jewson**. Coxswain Woods reported that the **Kara** was in distress about a mile from the **Corton** lightvessel station (the lightvessel had been mined earlier and was not on station). He also reported numerous floating mines. The **Kara** was towed out of the channel but broke in two and sank.

In November another minesweeper was in trouble. On the 18th the *Kentwell* was called to a vessel burning flares in Corton Roads. There was a gale force wind from ESE and she was towed out by a tug. By the time they got out the vessel, **HMS Northern Prince**, was on the beach and they could not get to her. The coastguards were there and had a line to her. The lifeboat stood by until all had been rescued and then returned to harbour.

The new year, 1917, started promptly when there was a call to the steamer **Rotterdam** aground on the Newcome on 1 January. She was not making any signals for help and since the Pakefield lifeboat had launched Coxswain

Swan and his men went home. The *James Leath* from Pakefield stood by the ship until she was refloated early next morning. Two GER tugs the **Despatch** and **Lowestoft** were awarded £715 for salvage, but there is no record of anything for the Pakefield men.

Not until August was there another call when on the 3rd the ketch **William Grant** which was being towed by a smack was seen to be flying a distress signal. The Coastguards called the lifeboat and John Swan got his men together and the boat Reserve 1A ready. By the time they were ready a Naval boat had taken the ketch in tow and the *Stock Exchange* stood down. Reserve 1A was Naval parlance for the *Stock Exchange*.

On 1 September they actually got out. The steamer **Yewdale** of Dundee went onto the NE Newcome. She was bound to France with pig iron. For the last time *Stock Exchange* was manned and went out. After a while the Captain decided to employ some help and asked the lifeboat to take a rope to the tug **Lowestoft** which was waiting nearby. After a while the ship came off and carried on her way. The salvage fee for this amounted to £500 with the lifeboat getting £210. This was a bit better than the miserly £25 paid by the Navy for getting off the new minesweeper in 1915.

This was the last launch of the *Stock Exchange* (Reserve 1A). The following year she was sent to Southwold, but rejected by the local crew and returned to Lowestoft. She was condemned in November 1918. She had launched 51 times and saved 40 lives at Lowestoft.

On 10 January 1918 the Norwegian steamer **Lars Lea** of Bergen ran onto Corton beach. Mr F Spashett, the Lloyd's Agent, asked Swan to lay out two anchors. Having obtained permission to take the lifeboat the *Kentwell* went out and laid the anchors. In due course £150 was received in salvage money.

September is often thought of as a good month for weather, but on the 30th of the month the lifeboat had a call which John Swan recorded as about the worst they ever had. There was a strong NE wind with heavy rain when in the early morning of the minesweeper **HMS Pomona** went ashore at Minsmere, south of Southwold. Major E R Cooper, Hon. Sec. of Southwold station was called at 2am. He rang the Aldeburgh station and the Coxswain there said he was unable to get off. Cooper decided then to try to launch the small Southwold boat *Rescue* (the bigger *Alfred Corry* had been condemned) but after several attempts to get a crew he had to tell the Naval Base at Lowestoft that he was unable to launch. Kessingland were also unable to get a crew. At this stage of the War there was an acute shortage of younger men and no doubt many stations experienced the same crew-finding difficulties. The Naval Station called John Swan and at first he said he could not get a crew, but later that he would try. After a while he managed to get 18 men - 4 over 50 years, 12 over 60 and 2 over 70! The *Kentwell* launched at 5am and proceeded under sail arriving at 7am. The difficult part then started.

The vessel was completely under water with four men on top of the wheelhouse and five on the foremast. Three had been washed off before the lifeboat arrived - two coming up on the beach but the third, the Master, was drowned. Swan attempted to get the lifeboat into the vessel, but did not succeed the first time, having brought the boat up into the wind she was then carried away on the tide. They then made an attempt to row to the wreck but heavy seas defeated them and also at a second try. Grappling irons were thrown into the rigging, these held and the boat was pulled towards the mast. Five men dropped one by one into the boat. One fell on William Butcher injuring Butcher's head slightly, the man fell overboard and was brought back smartly with a boathook. The lifeboat was hauled off by the cable to the wheelhouse. A line was thrown to the four men here, an endless rope made and they were hauled through the water to the lifeboat.

During the time they had been carrying all this out the lifeboat was often under water and hit the bottom more than once. They hauled away from the wreck and made sail for Lowestoft. Fortunately for everybody the tug **Despatch** arrived and took the *Kentwell* in tow. A minesweeper came up and ordered the men put aboard a Naval Patrol boat. Swan refused saying that he had risked boat and men to rescue them and he was not going to pass them onto another vessel. They arrived back at Lowestoft at 1045am having been out in an open boat for nearly six hours, without food, shelter or anywhere much even to sit. Swan reckoned it the worst trip for him thusfar. For this service he received a bar to his RNLI Silver medal and 30/-. The second Coxswain received a Bronze medal and 30/-. William Butcher for breaking the fall of a survivor and getting hurt got an additional 7/6d. Each man got a certificate. Swan recorded that they would all have liked a medal, except one!

So the Great War came to a close, during it Lowestoft lifeboats had saved 142 people.

Part II - The final years of Pulling and Sailing boats

In 1869 the Lowestoft No. 2 station opened with the arrival of the lifeboat *George* built at Beechings of Yarmouth. She saved five and was launched 6 times before being replaced in 1886. The second boat was *Two Sisters Mary and Hannah* which came from the Pakefield station. She saved 18 lives and was launched 11 times while at Lowestoft. In 1890 *The Stock Exchange* came to Lowestoft No. 2 station and saved five lives in 10 launches before being replaced in 1892 by a new boat called *Stock Exchange*. By the time the station closed in 1918 she had launched 51 times and saved 40 people.

The Great War had ended on 11 November 1918 and four days later the *Kentwell* was called to the Dutch sloop **Regina**. She had run onto the north part of the Newcome. To save time, a steam drifter patrol boat towed the lifeboat out, but by the time they reached the casualty she had knocked off into deep water and had anchored. Some lifeboatmen went on board and prepared a tow with one of the harbour tugs taking both lifeboat and dutchman into harbour.

On 20 December the *Kentwell* was towed out in a smart northerly breeze to the three masted schooner **Susan Vittery** of Grimsby which was firing rockets and burning flares having gone onto the Holm Sand. When the tide started to make she was found to be leaking badly so the Captain employed six boatmen who went on board to help with the pumping and to make the tow ready. She had a cargo of coal for France but this had to be discharged in Lowestoft before she went to the Acorn Shipyard at Rochester for a survey. She had broken her keel in three places and many flooring boards were broken. There was no slipway available at Rochester so she was towed to Whitstable where she was practically rebuilt. Soon afterwards her Master Captain Creenan bought her and renamed her **Brooklands**.

A week later on 27 December the hulk of the schooner **Mary Mackays** broke away from the tug which was towing her and ended up on the Holm Sand. The *Kentwell* went out and the Captain said he would leave her as she was leaking, so they rescued six and a dog bringing them into Lowestoft. During the night the hulk blew off and the following morning her own tug found her and remade the tow.

The first job of 1919 lasted five days. The French steamer **Parame** of Havre with a crew of 24 bound for Newcastle in ballast ran onto Corton Beach in a strong ExN wind with snow squalls and heavy seas.The *Kentwell* was towed down by the **Lowestoft**. As the lifeboat was getting ready to go alongside the recall signal was fired from the shore, the crew having already been landed. Two days later on 1 February Mr Spashett, the Lloyds Agent, asked Coxswain Swan to lay out anchors for the ship and so an agreement was made for £250. The anchors were duly laid out. Over the next three days four tugs attempted to get her off but failed. When they arrived at the scene on 4 February they found the sea had done much of the work for them and turned her head to sea. The tugs connected up again and soon had her off and into harbour. The GER records show that **Lowestoft** and **Despatch** were awarded £686 for salvage, the other two tugs being from Yarmouth. A beach gig was apparently used during this job since one features in the list of doles. She was probably used to go where the lifeboat could not.

On 3 May 1919 John Swan and George Ayers attended the Annual Meeting of the RNLI in London. Here they were presented with their medals for the service to the **Pomona** the previous September. There was a bar to his Silver medal for Swan and the Bronze medal for George Ayers. While they were away there was a call. This was to the small yacht **Pleiad** which had gone onto the Newcome. The *Kentwell* was taken out by the bowman John Rose but the skipper refused all help. They stood by in the heavy swell until she knocked over the sands.

November 15th 1919 was a day many Lowestoft people were to remember as they were able to see a difficult lifeboat rescue right under their noses. There was a strong ENE gale blowing with a heavy sea running as the steam drifter LT387 **Ocean's Gift** made for the harbour entrance. Unfortunately she was thrown off course by the heavy backwash off the North Extension and finished up on the sand bank on the south side of the South pier. Hearing the lifeboat maroons, hundreds of people made their way to the scene. The coastguards with the rocket apparatus under Chief Officer Clarke were also there. The tug **Lowestoft** towed the *Kentwell* out and the first job to was to get a wire from the vessel to the pier to stop her going further shorewards. After this Coxswain Swan went alongside and got the crew of nine. Heavy seas were breaking over the drifter and the *Kentwell* and during the rescue the outrigger on the lifeboat was broken and fell on the Coxswain injuring one of his legs.

While all this was going on the tug **Despatch** was towing in the ketch **Fiducia** of Hull and as they were entering harbour the tow rope broke. Another rope was quickly thrown from the South Pier which stopped her from drifting down on the **Ocean's Gift**. It so happened that when the crew were taken off the drifter her engines were left running and when she knocked off the bank she ran into the stern of the **Fiducia**. The crew were quickly put back on the drifter, the engines were stopped and she was towed into harbour. Meanwhile the **Fiducia** was being hauled round the pier head and drifters entering the harbour had to dodge her bowsprit, but one the **Recompense** had the bowsprit through her wheelhouse windows but was seen safely into harbour. The crowd on the Pier certainly had their money's worth as at the time the entrance fee was probably only 1d. The lifeboat went up to Chambers yard for repairs costing £6 7s.9d. The salvage money for her was £60.

This launch was yet further proof, if any were needed, that a motor lifeboat was urgently required. By a great coincidence at the Branch Committee meeting the previous day it was mentioned that money had been provided for just such a boat by Miss Agnes Cross of London. She had given the RNLI £6000 specifically for a boat for Lowestoft. She had been a regular visitor to the town always residing on Marine Parade and had no doubt watched the lifeboat go out many times.

On 23 November 1919 there was some competition for the lifeboat. The motor schooner **Ellen I** of Tonsberg had run onto the Newcome Sand while on her way to France. A pilot boat got there first followed by the Old Company's gig **Norah** and one from the Young Company the **United**. As the wind and tide made they had to come in and were replaced by the *Kentwell*. She took a rope to the **Despatch** which towed the schooner off on high water. In the Admiralty Court in April 1920 the tug was awarded £400, the pilot boat £60 and the two gigs £90 between them. There was apparently nothing for the lifeboat.

The lifeboat nearly became a casualty herself on 7 March 1920. At about 7.20pm the coastguards saw a vessel burning flares near the southern end of the Newcome. It was the drifter LT1096 **Retriever II** which had developed engine trouble on her way home. When nearing Lowestoft she became lost in a snowstorm and fired off distress signals. However the weather cleared, the engine settled down and so she continued on her way. The *Kentwell* had launched and met the drifter at the harbour mouth. The 'casualty' had to go hard astern to avoid a collision, and the lifeboat dropped her sail and escorted the drifter through the bridge to a mooring.

During the afternoon of 10 July John Swan was down near the Low Light when he saw the small two-handed trawler LT23 **Sydney and Ethel** in difficulties in the North Roads. The wind was against the tide and causing a nasty sea. The *Kentwell* was towed out by **Despatch** and found the casualty waterlogged near Corton. They took off the two men and towed the boat home. This may well have been the lifeboat's smallest ever 'customer'.

The Wilson Line ship **Albano** of Hull bound for the Mediterranean with 1200 tons of cargo ran aground on the Newcome on 2 October 1920 in a strong SW wind and heavy sea. The *Kentwell* sailed out at about 10.15am and spoke to her Master who asked them to stand by. An hour or so later he asked them to take a line to the tug **Lowestoft**. After about an hour the vessel came off, cast off from the tug and proceeded on her way. In February 1921 the Admiralty Court awarded the tug £750 and the lifeboat £250. There was some further legal argument and the lifeboat's portion was reduced to £237 10s.

A little poem commemorates the next casualty the smack LT167 **Belle**. She was homeward bound on 4 October when the wind fell light and she missed stays and drifted ashore on the North beach fouling the wreck of **HMS Spider**. The lifeboat crew mustered at about 4am but the wind had gone easterly and they had to wait for a tug which did not arrive until nearly 5am. By this time the crew of the smack had rowed their own boat ashore, and the vessel was wrecked. Later in the month her stores were auctioned by Messrs Hobsons at the LBS Engineering Co premises. The Board of Trade enquiry was held in April 1921 and the skipper had his certificate returned to him with £15 towards his expenses. At the time of the wreck he maintained he signalled for help but non came. After this enquiry someone wrote a poem which appeared in the *Lowestoft Journal*.

BELLES LETTRES

The skipper says he showed some flares
And toot tootled on his horn
But the coastguard on duty stoutly swears
That for pipe lights those lamps were borne

The cause of the loss of the good ship **Belle**
We may add (as a sort of rider)
Was the result of her dragging her hook like - well
And fouling the wreck of the **Spider**.

Later the same month near the Claremont Pier on 25 October the smack RX310 **Uncle Dick** dragged her anchor and was in danger of running onto some groynes. Coxswain Swan took the *Kentwell* out under sail, anchored and veered down to the vessel, took a tow rope and, hauling on the anchor, got the smack clear. The tug **Despatch** arrived and towed the lifeboat and the smack to harbour. The smack had anchored because while she was in Pakefield Gat the main gaff was broken.

The last time the *Kentwell* was prepared for service was on 28 January 1921 when the smack LT942 **Iris** went on the Newcome Sand. As the lifeboatmen were assembling they saw that the Pakefield boat had launched and so they stood down. So the service to **Uncle Dick** the previous October had been the last for the *Kentwell*.

In her 16 years at Lowestoft she launched 60 times and saved 168 lives.

About two weeks later the Gorleston station was closed and their boat was moved to Lowestoft. By a strange twist the *Kentwell* was taken to Gorleston in May the following year to re-open the station there.

The new boat was the *John and Mary Meiklam of Gladswood* which the RNLI took into service in early 1921 after she was built by S E Saunders of Cowes. On 16 April she undertook a trial trip at Lowestoft with a crew of 37. The list of their names makes interesting reading, there were 5 Swans, 4 Ayers, 3 Butchers, 3 Allertons and 3 Roses illustrating how lifeboating runs in families. During this trial Coxswain Swan tried out the new Schermuly line-throwing gun managing a 70 yard throw against the wind.

Her first call came on 27 September to the steam collier **Pollcrea** aground on the north end of the Newcome. The second Coxswain took the boat out, but the pilot boat beat her and was employed to save the ship. The beachmen jettisoned the deck cargo of coke and 60 tons of coal and she floated off on the evening of the following day, helped by the efforts of a large Gravesend tug.

Nearly a month later on 23 October the usefulness of a motor lifeboat was illustrated. The Coxswain of the Caister lifeboat telephoned Coxswain Swan at 6.45am to say a schooner was on the Barber Sand off the village. Neither the Caister nor Winterton boats could get off in the severe NE gale. John Swan roused out his crew of 15 and set off. They searched for some time but did not find the casualty the **Welsh Belle** of Falmouth. She had in fact knocked off into deep water and started to fill. The crew of four took to their boat and made for the shore where they were rescued from the breakers by people on the beach.

After this trip to Caister (12 miles away) John Swan reported that such a journey was too far because when they got there the men were exhausted and would not have been fit for any rescue work. However he said the boat behaved very well under a severe test.

In the spring of 1922 the *John and Mary Meiklam of Gladswood* was renamed *Agnes Cross* and rescued six men on the first service under her new name. On 14 June the Norwegian motor schooner **Kirstine** carrying sand from London to Grangemouth went on the Newcome. Later she came off after the crew had been saved and the tug **Lowestoft** tried to get a line to her but a strong northerly wind blew her ashore near the Grand Hotel (now the MAFF Fisheries Laboratory) and she was completely wrecked.

During October 1922 Coxswain Swan carried out what was arguably his finest service for which he was awarded the RNLI Gold medal. It was to the steamer **Hopelyn** aground on the north end of Scroby Sand near Yarmouth. To quote from his logbook.

"Called out Friday October 22nd at 4pm to go to Gorleston to pick up Inspector Carver (RNLI District Inspector). We arrived at 5pm, took Mr Carver and proceeded towards the wreck, but before we got there the Gorleston lifeboat *Kentwell* was coming away, so we spoke them, took off the Coxswain, and returned towards the wreck. I got such a poor account of the wreck that I decided to wait till daylight next morning, so we returned to Gorleston. We left at 4am and arrived at the wreck at 6am, let go the anchor, wore down to her, took off all the crew and a black cat. The poor fellows had been in the Marconi house, 12 foot square, for 36 hours. The Gorleston boat had tried to get to her for two days but could not do so. Blowing a gale from ENE with weather moderating (on Saturday). We landed the crew at Yarmouth up at the bridge. We got a great reception all the way up the river from fishing boats and the shore. When the crew got ashore the crowd gave us three hearty cheers. We left for home where we arrived at 8.15am. From the time we let go the anchor till we got the crew was 10 minutes, smart work. The Institution sent down 2 service calls one for Friday and one for Saturday. Friday night when we arrived at Gorleston we had to send five of our men home since they were Skippers and had to go to sea next day. So when we went for the crew of the **Hopelyn** we had seven of the Gorleston crew and 10 of ours."

An undramatic account of what must have been a nightmare for everybody concerned including the cat!

The Gorleston lifeboat was damaged while attempting the rescue and Coxswain Fleming advised Swan that it was dangerous to try during darkness since the sides of the vessel were split and jagged. The Lowestoft Secretary reported that "Knowing what he knows now, Swan would have tried on Friday evening rather than postponing till Saturday morning."

The District Inspector's report gave more details, in brief it is this:

"At about 9.45pm on 19 October the coastguards at Gorleston observed rockets to the NE and called Caister lifeboat. By 11pm it was apparent that Caister could not launch and so at 11.10pm Gorleston No.1 lifeboat launched and in tow of a tug made towards the wreck. On arrival the Coxswain decided to wait for daylight and so he lay off. When dawn came only the mid-ships portion of the vessel was above water, with heavy seas breaking right over it and no sign of life. They arrived back at Gorleston at 9am. About an hour later the coastguard at Caister reported flags being shown from the wreck, and so the Gorleston boat *Kentwell* returned to the site. They lay near the wreck and anchored."

The District Inspector could see all this from the Gorleston Coastguard lookout and by 3.30pm he concluded that the Gorleston boat could not get near. He therefore called Lowestoft with instructions to collect him on the way. His reports goes on:

"When the Gorleston Coxswain was taken on board he explained that terrific seas, broken portions of the hull and the remains of an old wreck prevented him getting alongside."

He went on later to describe the scene on Saturday:

"Only the bridge and casing were above water with the fore and aft decks submerged and the hull split fore and aft of the bridge with jagged plates projecting. There was barely a clear lifeboat-length to come alongside. Whilst veering down the lifeboat was struck by an enormous sea and almost thrown onto the after deck. Had it not been for the powerful motor in the boat I do not consider we could have got alongside. It took only 30 seconds for all the crew to jump into us and we were forced to cut away the anchor which was foul of an old wreck. At the same time the lifeboat was buried in a huge broadside sea, but nobody was thrown out."

The **Hopelyn** was from Newcastle bound for London with 3400 tons of coal.

For this rescue both John Swan of Lowestoft and Coxswain William Fleming of Gorleston received the RNLI Gold medal with the Gorleston and Lowestoft crew members receiving the Bronze one and the Lowestoft Mechanic and the Lifeboat Inspector Silver medals. Later, in 1924 Coxswains Swan and Fleming were each invested with the OBE by King George V at Buckingham Palace. This was after John Swan had retired in June 1924 aged 67, having carried out a further 14 services after the **Hopelyn**.

His last call had been to the **Corton** lightvessel on 26 February 1924. One of her crew had fallen from the mast and had been killed, so the Master fired his guns. The dead man was taken off by a Yarmouth drifter while the *Agnes Cross* was on her way.

During his time as Coxswain John Swan had launched over 90 times and had saved 290 people, two cats and one dog.

He died in Lowestoft Hospital on 20 February 1935 aged 78 and was buried in St. Margaret's Churchyard with six lifeboatmen acting as bearers. He was reported to have been involved in saving a total of 407 lives during his service as crewmember and Coxswain.

In the *Lowestoft Journal* of 26 February 1965 (exactly 41 years after his last service) an interesting article appeared. It reported the imminent demolition of a row of Fishermen's Almshouses in Whapload Road which was part of the old beach village. One of them was Hopelyn Cottage where John Swan lived after he retired until his death. This cottage and one at the other end of the row were given to the Lowestoft Charity Board in 1907 by Mr T E Thirtle, a drifter owner, as a thankoffering for a good fishing season.

Table 4

Services under Coxswain Swan 1911 - 1924

1911 *Kentwell*

19 Mar	trawler, **Express** (LT73), S Roads	ns
	Stock Exchange	
21 Apr	yacht, **Ariba** of Ramsgate	ns
4 Aug	small boat off Corton	ns
28 Oct	drifter, **Boy Willie** (LT527), N Beach	stood by
	Kentwell	
13 Dec	ss **Poplar** of London, Newcome	ns

1912 *Kentwell*

16 Apr	smack, **Qui Vive** (LT702), S Pier	assembly
	Stock Exchange	
16 May	smack, **Gladiolus** (LT291), N Extension	stood by
4 Sep	m.yacht, **Muriel** of Lowestoft, Newcome	saved 3
	Kentwell	
25 Nov	smack, **Emmanuel** (LT169), Newcome	assisted

1913 *Kentwell*

11 Jan	barge, **Alice Watts** of Harwich, N Roads	assisted
	barge, **Gladys** of Dover, N Roads	saved 3
12 Jan	barge, **Gladys** of Dover, N Roads	saved vessel
27 Jan	smack, **Pet** (LT560), Newcome	saved vessel
4 Apr	smack, **Evolution** (LT1033), N Beach	assisted
19Apr	small boat from **Pet** (LT560), Holm	saved 1
10 Jun	longshore fb, **Surprise** (LT625)	assisted
3 Sep	trawler, **Eugene Elvire** of Ostend, Newcome	assisted

1914 *Kentwell*

14 Feb	smack, **Wave Crest** (LT744), N Pier	assisted
	smack, **Comrades** (LT315), Harbour Bar	assisted
	smack, **Active** (LT513), Harbour Bar	assisted
15 Oct	Belgian trawlers with refugees, Newcome	saved 35
21 Oct	smack, **Emmanuel** (LT169), Newcome	assisted
11 Nov	ss **Olga** of Esbjerg, Holm	stood by
22 Nov	**HMS Spider**, N Beach	saved 13
	HMS Condor, Newcome	saved 9
26 Nov	ss **F Stobart** of Sunderland, Holm	stood by
11 Dec	missing naval cutter	ns
14 Dec	smack, **Boy Claude** (LT84), N Extension	took off 4
31 Dec	**HMS Jay**, S Roads	stood by

1915 *Kentwell*

2 Feb	barge, **Sirdar** of Grays, Newcome	saved 2
15 Mar	ms **San Ricardo**, Corton Sand	ns
	Stock Exchange	
18 Apr	ss **Glenpark** of Greenock, Holm	assisted
27 May	**HMS Canton**, Newcome	assisted
13 Aug	ss **Sverige** of Gefle, Stanford Channel	saved 3
	Kentwell	
27 Oct	ss **Gar de Pee** of Cardiff, Holm	saved 22
28 Oct	ss **Gar de Pee** of Cardiff, Holm	assisted
2 Nov	mb **Meg** of Lowestoft, Newcome	ns
8 Nov	ss **Loch Lomond** of Dundee, Holm	assisted
9 Nov	ss **Loch Lomond** of Dundee, Holm	assisted
10 Nov	ss **Loch Lomond** of Dundee, Holm	assisted
13 Nov	ketch, **Mientze** of London, N Beach	ns
29 Nov	ss **Framfield** of London, Newcome	saved 24
30 Nov	ss **Framfield** of London, Newcome	assisted
1 Dec	ss **Framfield** of London, Newcome	assisted
26 Dec	ss **Wharfdale** of Sunderland, Newcome	stood by

1916 *Kentwell*

23 Feb	schooner, **Carmenta** of Whitstable, Thorpeness	ns
28 Mar	five ships on Corton Beach	ns
29 Mar	schooner on Corton Beach	ns
	HMS Blacklyn, Corton Beach	assisted
	Stock Exchange	
10 Jul	ss **Kara** of London, Pakefield Gat	saved 21
	Kentwell	
18 Nov	**HMS Northern Prince**, Corton Beach	ns

1917 *Kentwell*

1 Jan	ss **Rotterdam** of Goole, Newcome	assembled
	Stock Exchange	
3 Aug	ketch, **William Grant**, N Roads	assembled
28 Aug	ss **Nimrod** of London, N Roads	ns
1 Sep	ss **Yewdale** of Dundee, Newcome	assisted

1918 *Kentwell*

10 Jan	ss **Lars Lea** of Bergen, Corton	assisted
30 Sep	**HMS Pomona**, Dunwich	saved 9
15 Nov	sloop **Regina** of Rotterdam, Newcome	assisted
20 Dec	schooner, **Susan Vittery** of Grimsby, Holm	assisted
27 Dec	schooner, **Mary Mackays** of Grimsby, Holm	saved 6 + dog

1919 *Kentwell*

30 Jan	ss **Parame** of Havre, Corton Beach	ns
1 Feb	ss **Parame** of Havre, Corton Beach	assisted
3 May	yacht, **Pleiad**, Newcome	stood by
15 Nov	drifter, **Ocean's Gift** (LT387), S Pier	saved 9
	ketch, **Fiducia** of Hull, S Pier	stood by
	drifter, **Ocean's Gift** (LT387), S Pier	assisted
23 Nov	schooner, **Ellen I** of Tonsberg, Newcome	ns
	schooner, **Ellen I** of Tonsberg, Newcome	assisted

1920 *Kentwell*

7 Mar	drifter, **Retriever II** (LT1096), Newcome	assisted
14 Apr	smack, **Proceed** (LT490), N Extension	assembled
10 Jul	longshore, **Sydney and Ethel** (LT23), N Roads	saved 2 + vessel
2 Oct	ss **Albano** of Hull, Newcome	assisted
4 Oct	smack, **Belle** (LT167), N Beach	assembled
25 Oct	smack, **Uncle Dick** (RX310), S Roads	assisted

1921 *Kentwell*

28 Jan	smack, **Iris** (LT942), Newcome	assembled

John and Mary Meiklam of Gladswood

27 Sep	ss **Pollcrea** of London, Newcome	assisted
23 Oct	schooner, **Welsh Belle** of Falmouth, Barber Sand	ns
6 Nov	hulk, **Crocus** of Hull, N Roads	saved 4
22 Nov	drifter, **Silverford** (BF353), N Extension	saved 7
24 Nov	drifter, **Spider** (BF279), Yarmouth Roads	ns
29 Nov	**Corton** LV, signals from	ns
26 Dec	trawler, **Halifax** (GY442), N Beach	saved 10

1922 *John and Mary Meiklam of Gladswood*

12 Jan	ss **Dalton** with survivors from ss **Tidal**	took off 15
19 Jan	trawler, **Electric** (GY286), harbour mouth	saved 9
27 Jan	trawler, **Whitby** (GY524), N Beach	stood by
2 Feb	smack, **Thyme** (LT1222), N Extension	assembled

Agnes Cross

14 Jun	schooner, **Kirstine** of Sandnes, Newcome	saved 6
17 Oct	smack, **Acme** (LT651), S Beach	saved 5
20 Oct	ss **Hopelyn** of Newcastle, Scroby Sand	ns
21 Oct	ss **Hopelyn** of Newcastle, Scroby Sand	saved 24 + cat
24 Oct	drifter, **Lovedale** (BF654), N Beach	saved 9
1 Nov	drifter, **Accumulator** (LT655), N Extension	assembled
10 Nov	drifter, **Rubicon** (BCK200), N Extension	assembled

1923 *Agnes Cross*

2 Jan	smack, **Louise** (LT388), Newcome	escorted
9 Feb	ss **Linhope** of Newcastle, Holm	assisted
16 Apr	fb **Burgemeister Ripping,** of Holland, N Beach	assisted
16 Jun	shrimper, **Boy Arthur** (LT1213), S Roads	saved 2 + vessel
3 Oct	small boat **White Bud** overdue	ns
23 Oct	drifter, **Jean II** of Boulogne, Newcome	saved 28
24 Nov	drifter, **Lord Curzon** (LT7), N Beach	stood by
5 Dec	ss **Prosper** of Germany, Holm	ns

1924 *Agnes Cross*

9 Jan	smack, **Irene** (LT976), S Pier	saved 5 + cat
12 Jan	barge, **Runic** of London, Holm	stood by
26 Feb	**Corton** LV, crewman killed	ns

Coxswain John Swan, he was in charge of Lowestoft
lifeboats from 1911 until 1924.
(*PLRS Collection*)

The New Young Company's beach yawl **Georgiana**, of which John Swan was at one time Coxswain.

(*PLRS Collection*)

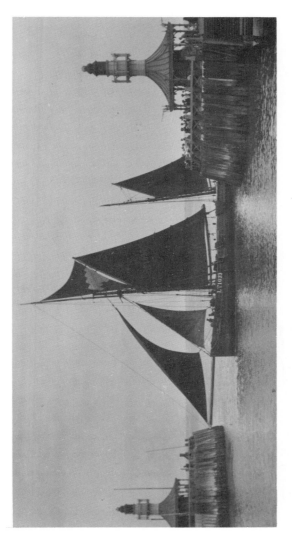

The sailing smack **Evolution** (LT1033) seen here entering Lowestoft harbour. On 4 April 1913 she was towed off the North beach with the help of the lifeboat. (*PLRS Collection*)

Wreck of the "Carmenta", Sizewell, Feb. 23. 16

The schooner **Carmenta** of Faversham ashore at
Sizewell, to which the Lowestoft lifeboat was called
even though smaller ones could not get near. Note the
man being rescued by breeches buoy, as were all the
crew on 23 February 1916.

(Photo by J S Waddell of Leiston, from the PLRS Collection)

RNLB **Kentwell** rescuing the crew of the steam drifter
Ocean's Gift (LT387) ashore on Lowestoft South
beach 15 November 1919.
(*PLRS Collection*)

RNLB *Agnes Cross* (ON663), stationed at Lowestoft from 1921 until 1939.

(W Keith Collection)

The steam drifter **Accumulator** (LT655) aground at the entrance to Lowestoft harbour 1 November 1922. The crew were saved by the lifeboat crew using ropes from the pier.
(*PLRS Collection*)

APPENDIX 1

COXSWAINS

ROBERT WILLIAM HOOK 1853-1883

'Bob' Hook was born on 4 June 1828 and joined the lifeboat crew in the 1840's. He was appointed Coxswain in 1853 by a majority vote of the members of the Beach Companies who provided the crews for the Lifeboat which at that time was managed by The Suffolk Humane Society. Control of the Lifeboat passed to the RNLI in 1855.

Hook was twice awarded the RNLI Silver medal; firstly for a service to the ss **Shamrock** on 1 November 1859 and secondly for rescuing 10 men from the brig **Expedite** on 13 November 1872. Both of these services were detailed by Jack Mitchley in Part 1.

After he retired from the RNLI in 1883 he became Coxswain of the private Lifeboat *Carolina Hamilton.*

Bob Hook died in 1911 at the age of 83.

WILLIAM JENNER CAPPS 1883-1901

William Capps was born 19 October 1840 and following the retirement of Bob Hook became Coxswain on 17 January 1883.

However, he had made his first service call just before then when he went to two ketches the **Wonderful** and the **John and Mary** on 9 January 1883.

He died while still in service in 1901 at the age of 60 having saved over 100 lives in 18 years.

JOHN MEWSE 1901-1911

On 13 March 1901 John Mewse was appointed Coxswain and carried out his first service call later that month on the 30th to the schooner **Elizabeth**.

He retired in January 1911 on reaching the RNLI retirement age, having in his 10 years as Coxswain saved 34 lives.

JOHN THOMPSON STERRY SWAN 1911-1924

John Swan was appointed to succeed John Mewse and served until 1924 having saved over 290 lives. His first service was to the trawler **Express** on 19 March 1911.

He was awarded the RNLI Silver medal for a service on 22 November 1914 to two minesweepers **HMS Spider** and **HMS Condor** saving 22 people in the process. Later he was awarded a second Silver medal for a service to **HMS Pomona** on 30 September 1918 when nine people were saved.

In April 1921 he became Coxswain of the first motor lifeboat on the Lowestoft station. On 20 October 1922 he took part in a particularly difficult service to rescue 24 crew from the collier **Hopelyn** on the north Scroby Sands. He was deservedly awarded only the second RNLI Gold medal to come to Lowestoft.

Coxswain Swan retired in June 1924 aged 67 and on the 30th of that month, with six other Lifeboat Gold medallists, was received by King George V at Buckingham Palace where he was invested with the insignia of the Most Excellent Order of the British Empire. He was presented with the RNLI Gold badge in April 1930 for his fund raising work for the RNLI.

He died on 20 February 1935 aged 78 and was buried in St. Margaret's Churchyard, Lowestoft with six crew members acting as bearers.

BOAT DETAILS

No. 1 Station

Samuel Plimsoll (ON22) 1867-1905. 83 launches, 165 saved.

Built by S Sparham on the North beach at Lowestoft at a cost of £276. She was launched by Mr Plimsoll who was an MP for Derby where funds had been raised for the boat which was a gift of the Samuel Plimsoll Lifeboat Fund.
A wooden pulling and sailing boat 14 oars 44ft x 12ft

Kentwell (ON543) 1905-21. 60 launches, 168 saved.

Built by Thames Ironworks, London at a cost of £2197 from a legacy of Mrs E A Moore of London.
A wooden pulling and sailing boat 14 oars 46ft x 12ft 6inches

Agnes Cross (ON663) 1921-39. 124 launches, 209 saved.

Built by S E Saunders, Cowes, IoW as the *John and Mary Meiklam of Gladswood* at a cost of £8620 for the Gorleston station being transferred to Lowestoft in late 1921. She was renamed in 1922 and appropriated to the gift of Miss Agnes F Cross of South Kensington, London.
A wooden motor lifeboat 46ft 9inches x 12ft 10inches with a 60 bhp Tylor engine.

No. 2 Station

George (ON-) 1870-81. 6 launches, 5 saved.

Built by Beeching Bros, Great Yarmouth at a cost of £156. A gift from Miss Mary Ann Leicester of Bayswater, London, who launched the boat and named it after her brother.
A wooden pulling and sailing boat 12 oars 32ft x 10ft

This boat opened the No. 2 station for inshore work since it had been found that the *Samuel Plimsoll* was too big for use under oars close inshore.
The station was closed between 1881 and 1886.

Two Sisters Mary and Hannah (ON23) 1886-90. 11 launches, 18 saved.

She was built in 1872 by S Sparham for the Pakefield No.1 station at a cost of £291 from the legacy of Thomas Parkin of Wigton, Cumberland. She was transferred to Lowestoft when the Pakefield station was closed by sand and shingle being piled up at the boat house by tidal action.
A wooden pulling and sailing boat 14 oars 46ft 3inches x 12ft

The Stock Exchange (ON288) 1890-92. 10 launches, 5 saved.

Built by W T Ellis on the north beach at Lowestoft at a cost of £373. A gift from the Stock Exchange Lifeboat Fund.
A wooden pulling and sailing boat 14 oars 46ft 6inches x 12ft 9inches
She was transferred to Gorleston 1892 because the Lowestoft crew did not like her.

Stock Exchange (ON356) 1893-1918. 51 launches, 40 saved

Built by Beeching Bros, Great Yarmouth at a cost of £530, a gift from the Stock Exchange Lifeboat Fund.
A wooden pulling and sailing boat 14 oars 46ft x 12ft 9inches
She was condemned as unfit in November 1918 and the station was closed.

INDEX TO LIFEBOATS

INDEX TO VESSELS

brig	Expedite	67
trawler	Express (LT73)	45, 63, 68
smack	Eyrie (LT1121)	47
fb	Faith (Lowestoft)	34
drifter	Faithful (INS262)	44
tug	Fastnet	51
schooner	Fides (Nyborg)	32
ketch	Fiducia (Hull)	56, 57, 65
schooner	Fiducia (Germany)	46
schooner	Florence Louise (Hull)	34
ss	Framfield (London)	51, 64
trawler	Frobisher (YH1029)	43
fb	Frolic (LT296)	33
ss	F Stobart (Sunderland)	63
ss	Gangeren (Norway)	46
ss	Gar de Peё (Cardiff)	50, 64
tug	George Jewson (Yarmouth)	51, 52
smack	Gladiolus (LT291)	63
barge	Gladys (Dover)	45, 46, 63
ss	Glenpark (Greenock)	49, 64
yawl	Georgiana (Lowestoft)	45
ss	Gorm (Copenhagen)	1, 20
HMS	Halcyon	39, 47, 48
trawler	Halifax (GY442)	65
schooner	Hannah (Fowey)	24, 33
schooner	Hannah (Yarmouth)	32
brig	Harkaway (Shoreham)	17, 20
	Harry and Ernest	20
schooner	Hinderika Grietje Almina (Emden)	4
smack	Hiram (LT302)	26, 33
HMS	Hogue	47
brig	Hope (Hartlepool)	1, 20
schooner	Hope (Rye)	4
ss	Hopelyn (Newcastle)	60, 62, 65, 68
tug	Imperial (Lowestoft)	3, 17, 23, 28, 30, 39, 49, 50
smack	Industry (LT394)	38, 43
smack	Integrity (LT930)	44

drifter	Ocean's Gift (LT387)	56, 65
ss	Olga (Esbjerg)	63
smack	Olive Branch (LT258)	32
ss	Parame (Havre)	55, 65
lugger	Paramount (Hopeman)	24, 33
trawler	Paula Bertha (Ostend)	43
smack	Peace (LT286)	33
lugger	Pet (LT132)	20
smack	Pet (LT560)	63
sloop	Pilot	43
barge	Pioneer (Rochester)	42, 44
ss	Pittan (Russia)	44
yacht	Pleiad	56, 65
ss	Pollcrea (London)	59, 65
brigantine	Polka (Maldon)	3
HMS	Pomona	53, 56, 64, 68
ss	Poplar (London)	63
smack	Proceed (LT490)	65
smack	Progress (Lowestoft)	20
brig	Prosper (Carnarvon)	9, 13
ss	Prosper (Germany)	66
ketch	QED (Dartmouth)	5, 8, 9, 11, 13
smack	Qui Vive (LT702)	63
tug	Rainbow (Lowestoft)	3, 5, 22-30
drifter	Recompense	57
schooner	Regina (Jersey)	30, 34
sloop	Regina (Rotterdam)	55, 64
fb	Reliance	44
tug	Resolute (Lowestoft)	30, 40, 49
drifter	Retriever II (LT1096)	57, 65
sloop	Richard and Francis (Goole)	33
ss	Rotterdam (Goole)	52, 64
drifter	Rubicon (BCK200)	65
	Ruby	44
barge	Runic (London)	66
brig	Runo (Whitby)	9
	Ryhope (Hartlepool)	12

schooner	Topaz	34
fb	Trial	9
smack	Uncle Dick (RX310)	59, 65
tug	Undaunted	1
smack	Undine (LT289)	32
gig	United	57
tug	United Services	38
smack	Viator	41
brig	Warrior Queen (Whitby)	9
smack	Wave Crest (LT744)	63
schooner	Welsh Belle (Falmouth)	59, 65
ss	Wharfdale (Sunderland)	51, 64
trawler	Whitby (GY524)	65
fb	White Bud	66
tug	Wild Rose	41
ss	Wilfred Lawson	32
brigantine	Wilhelmina (Exeter)	17, 20
ketch	William Grant	53, 64
brigantine	William Thrift (Dundee)	6, 13, 18
ketch	Wonderful (Goole)	21, 32, 67
ss	Yewdale (Dundee)	53, 64
smack	Young Harry (LT288)	44
	Zenobia (Yarmouth)	11
brig	Zosteria (Colchester)	1, 20